A Thanks to Loneliness

Embracing the Beauty of Solitude
& finding the Strength Within

Mary Bridget O'Brien

A Thanks to Loneliness

Copyright © 2023 Mary Bridget O'Brien

All rights reserved.

ISBN: 13: 979-8-3879-6055-0

DEDICATION

To my children, who are the greatest treasures of my life, I am so proud of each one of you.

To my brothers and sisters, thank you for the memories we have shared and the bond we have created. Thanks for being there when times were tough.

To all of my dear friends, who have stood by me through thick and thin, and for always offering a listening ear and a kind word. Your loyalty and friendship mean the world to me, and I am blessed to have you in my life.

With love and gratitude.

A Thanks to Loneliness

A Thanks to Loneliness

CONTENTS

	Prologue	1
	Introduction	4
1	UNDERSTANDING LONELINESS *Exploring its Causes and Effects*	Pg 10
2	LEARNING TO LOVE YOURSELF *Building Self-Love and Acceptance*	Pg 18
3	OVERCOMING NEGATIVE SELF-TALK *How to Silence your Inner Critic*	Pg 24
4	MINDFULNESS AND MEDITATION *The Power of the Present Moment*	Pg 30
5	COGNITIVE RESTRUCTURING *Rewiring your Brain for Positive Change*	Pg 37
6	SELF-COMPASSION *Learning to Treat Yourself with Kindness*	Pg 48
7	NURTURING YOUR INNER CHILD *Reconnecting with that Beautiful Part of Yourself*	Pg 56
8	CULTIVATING POSITIVE RELATIONSHIPS	Pg 65

How to connect with others

9	MANAGING SOCIAL ANXIETY	Pg 80
	How to Overcome Fear and Isolation	
10	THE ART OF PRACTICING FORGIVENESS	Pg 85
	How Letting Go can Improve your Life	
11	PERFECTIONISM	Pg 93
	The Gift of being Perfectly Imperfect	
12	EMBRACING VULNERABILITY	Pg 99
	How to open up and connect	
13	THE MISPERCEPTION OF BEING STRONG	Pg 109
	Breaking the Illusion	
14	BREAKING THE HABIT OF SAYING 'NO'	Pg 115
	Unlocking Opportunities	
15	BUILDING A POSITIVE SELF-IDENTITY	Pg 122
	Developing a Stronger Sense of Self	
16	FINDING YOUR PASSION AND PURPOSE	Pg 136
	How to Live a Meaningful Life	
17	PRACTICING GRATITUDE	Pg 144

The Transformative Power of Appreciation

18 SEEKING PROFESSIONAL HELP   Pg 151
    How Therapy can Help you Overcome Loneliness

19 MAINTAINING LONG-TERM WELLBEING   Pg 156
    How to Build a Supportive Lifestyle

A Thanks to Loneliness

A Thanks to Loneliness

A Thanks to Loneliness

PROLOGUE

"Loneliness is not a misfortune, it's a gift. It's the opportunity to get to know yourself, to learn how strong you really are, and to appreciate everything and everyone else in your life." – Unknown

It's possible that you're reading this book because you're going through a difficult time and experiencing the painful feelings of loneliness. I understand that feeling all too well and want you to know that I'm here with you and feel your pain.

However, have you considered the idea of embracing loneliness instead of wishing it away?

When we experience loneliness, it can feel like a burden that we desperately want to rid ourselves of. However, what if we were to shift our perspective and view it as an opportunity for growth? By sitting with the pain and acknowledging its presence, we can begin to explore the deeper meaning behind our loneliness.

What if the key to overcoming loneliness isn't just about finding more friends or improving our social skills? What if the real solution lies in learning to love and accept ourselves?

Perhaps this experience is happening for a higher reason - to teach us a lesson, to help us develop greater empathy for others, or to push us out of our comfort zones and into new experiences. Instead of resisting and wishing for the feeling to go away, we can choose to embrace it and see it as a chance for personal growth.

Of course, personal growth doesn't necessarily require seeking out loneliness - there are many challenges and struggles in life that can teach us important lessons. However, when we do experience loneliness, we can choose to confront it directly and use it as an opportunity for self-reflection and growth.

By embracing loneliness, we can gain valuable insights into ourselves and our lives, learn to rely on ourselves more fully, and even develop a greater appreciation for the relationships and connections we do have in our lives.

So let us give thanks to loneliness. Let us embrace it as a valuable part of our lives, and allow it to guide us towards deeper self-awareness, creativity and connection.

A Thanks to Loneliness

INTRODUCTION

"Cultivate the habit of being alone without feeling lonely; embrace solitude and cherish your own company. It is in this space that true growth and self-discovery can occur." - Mandy Hale

As I write this book, I find myself in solitude because my daughter is spending the week with her dad leaving me to my own devices. Yet, as I glance over my shoulder, I do not see loneliness lurking nearby. It knows better than to waste its time with me, for I have learned not to entertain its presence. Instead, I am basking in the warm waters of contentment, revelling in the beauty of this solitary moment. It is a far cry from the painful loneliness I used to endure, and I am grateful for the peace that now surrounds me.

This current state of contentment and comfort in solitude is a stark contrast to the past, which was plagued with the opposite. At one point, the pain of loneliness was all-consuming and the idea of being alone was unbearable. But through personal growth and experience, I have come to a place where being alone is not only manageable, but also enjoyable.

Although I am grateful for the lessons I learned during my time of loneliness, I must admit that while I was going through it, the last thing on my mind was being thankful for it. It was a painful and difficult experience, and I felt lost, disconnected, and overwhelmed. But as I look back on that time in my life, I see now that there were hidden blessings in the loneliness that I couldn't see at the time. It forced me to confront parts of myself that I had been avoiding, and it gave me the space and time I needed to heal and grow. So while I didn't feel grateful for it at the time, I am now able to see the value in that difficult experience and appreciate it for what it taught me.

In many ways, it feels like loneliness has been hovering in the background my whole life, waiting for a vulnerable moment to strike.

The first time it truly floored me was when I divorced after twenty-two years of marriage. This was almost eighteen years ago, a different time when loneliness was still stigmatized and not commonly discussed. As a result, I felt ashamed of my feelings and kept them hidden, believing that others would think less of me if they found out.

Despite having a supportive network of family and friends, I still felt deeply alone and isolated, especially when I closed the door to my home.

I was now a single mother, and I felt a sense of emptiness that was difficult to shake. Sundays were especially tough, as it seemed like everyone else was surrounded by loved ones, while I was left on my own. I would often have the urge to reach out and ask if anyone wanted to do something, but I was afraid of being seen as a burden or an intruder. In my mind, I thought that others would see my loneliness as a sign of weakness or that there was something wrong with me.

During this time, I made the mistake of entering into a romantic relationship as a means of escaping the pain. So you can imagine I did not make a wise choice. Sure how could I make a wise decision when I was not in a good place with myself. *(I explore the pitfalls on starting a romantic relationship to escape loneliness later on.)*

For a period of ten years we were together, eight years as boyfriend and girlfriend, followed by two years as a married couple.

After my second marriage ended I found myself back in a similar situation, experiencing a profound sense of solitude once again.

But this time was different. I realized that if I was experiencing loneliness for the second time after separation, there must be others out there going through the same thing.

When I first separated at the age of forty in 2005, I personally knew nobody in Ireland who was separated or divorced. At that time, divorce was still a relatively new concept in Ireland due to the recent change in the law. However, ten years later, things had changed, and I no longer felt alone in my struggles.

Despite finding comfort in the fact that I was not alone in my struggles, I ultimately realized that the only person who could truly help me was myself. Although loneliness was the emotion I was experiencing on the surface, I knew that it was deeply ingrained within me, requiring a more profound form of self-care.

With this awareness, I made a conscious decision to take proactive steps towards healing and fulfilment, determined to overcome the emotional pain and find a sense of contentment within myself.

While everyone's experience with loneliness is unique, I understand the feelings of sadness and disconnection that can come with it.

Through my own personal journey, I have learned strategies to cope with loneliness and have found ways to connect with others. I hope that sharing my own experiences can provide some comfort to those of you who are going through the same thing.

As you read this book, I'll be sharing practical tips and insights to help you navigate the complex experience of loneliness. But I also want to offer you additional resources to aid you on your journey. Throughout the book, I'll be recommending books that have been personally impactful for me, and I encourage you to explore them further. These resources will provide you with a variety of tools and perspectives to help you overcome loneliness and find greater connection in your life.

My sincere hope for this book is that it provides you with the insights and tools necessary to understand and overcome your struggles with loneliness, and for it to serve as a guide and a companion on your journey towards a happier and more connected future.

My greatest wish is that you may embark on a path towards a more fulfilling and joyful life, unencumbered by the burdens of loneliness.

And maybe someday you will be able to look

back and feel so thankful for having gone through it.

1.. UNDERSTANDING LONELINESS
Exploring its Causes and Effects

"Loneliness is not a curse, but a gift. It allows us to discover who we truly are and what we are capable of." – Unknown

I have learned that loneliness is a really complicated feeling that's about way more than just being physically alone. It is a deep sense of disconnection and isolation that can make us feel like something important is missing in our lives.

It is not the same as enjoying our own company, which many of us find fulfilling. It is even possible to find enjoyment in our own company at times while experiencing loneliness.

Loneliness is different because it comes with a feeling of emptiness and a sense of not belonging.

As humans, we have a natural tendency to be social creatures and connect with others. This is something that's ingrained in us from the very beginning. Throughout history, we've always lived in groups and communities because we needed each other for survival, safety, and even reproduction.

Our brains are wired to crave social connection which is a fundamental part of being human. It doesn't matter if it's through close relationships, friendships, or even just casual acquaintances, we all need some level of social interaction to feel happy, healthy, and fulfilled.

There are lots of different things that can make us feel lonely. Maybe we don't have many close relationships, or we've lost someone we loved. Maybe we feel like we don't have a clear sense of purpose or direction in life. Or perhaps we find ourselves in an unhappy relationship leading us to feel lonely even while being in it.

Whatever the reason, loneliness can be something that we feel for a little while or for a long time. It is something that can happen to anyone.

Culture and society also play a big role in how we feel. Our society has changed a lot over time. Cities have become bigger, and more people live in really crowded areas. Because of this, it's not as easy to find close-knit communities, like neighbourhoods, where everyone knows each other.

Nowadays, things are very different. We are living in a time where the sense of community has changed significantly. The way we live and work has changed, and people are often spread out across different areas.

My mind often wanders back to my childhood in Dublin during the 1960s and 1970s, where community played an important role in my life. While I recognize that this was a time when it was more common for mothers to stay at home while their husbands worked, it was also a time when people looked out for each other, creating a tightly knit community.

Where I lived, children filled the streets with laughter and games. Whenever one of the mothers needed to run errands, or even go to the hospital to deliver a baby, the rest of the mothers would come together to take care of the children. I also recall an elderly lady who lived alone on our street. The women in our community would take turns checking in on her, bringing her meals and inviting her to their homes for dinner. It was a time when people genuinely cared for each other, regardless of whether they were related or close friends.

Although I may look back on this time through rose-tinted glasses, the sense of community and support that I experienced is something that has stayed with me throughout my life.

But, I feel that for us to truly understand loneliness, it's so important for us to acknowledge, and realize, that we are not the only ones who may be dealing with challenges in life.

I recall how, when feeling lonely, it appeared as if everyone else around me was happy, satisfied, and connected in their lives. This perception only intensified my feelings of disconnection and inadequacy. It's all too easy to become stuck in the notion that others have attained their dream job, perfect relationship, or ideal social circle. I genuinely believed that I was the only one experiencing loneliness among my friends and family.

However, this perception is false. Many people are adept at masking their own loneliness or presenting a filtered version of their lives to others, just like I did.

People are often taken aback when they hear I struggled because they see me as confident, strong, and assumed I was doing great. We don't often see the internal struggles, the heartbreaks, and the moments of isolation that others are experiencing.

Then there is social media which has given us the gift of being able to connect with friends from all over the world. However, while it's fun to see what others are up to on social media, unfortunately, it can often contribute to a false sense of reality.

People tend to present only their most positive experiences and emotions online, creating an illusion of perfection that doesn't necessarily exist in reality.

I remember the days scrolling through social media and watching as others appeared to be connected and happy, which made me feel even more isolated and alone. Of course, I have since learnt that this is a common issue experienced by many but, at the time I believed it was unique to me.

It's very important for us to remember that everyone struggles with loneliness at some point in their lives, and that no one is immune to going through challenges. When we acknowledge that feeling lonely is something that many people experience, we can begin to break down the barriers of isolation and create a sense of togetherness and bonding that can help us overcome life's challenges.

Lastly, since this book emphasizes the importance of embracing loneliness as a means to propel us towards personal growth and greater accomplishments, it is important to realize that it truly possesses the ability to initiate transformative change.

Based on my own personal experience, experiencing loneliness has given me the opportunity to connect with myself in ways I never imagined.

I have had numerous realizations and breakthroughs that I know would not have occurred if I wasn't experiencing loneliness. I have learned that, while loneliness can bring about feelings of disconnection and isolation, it can also be something that we choose to embrace.

Being alone and feeling lonely has given me the chance to reflect on my thoughts and emotions without the distractions of others. This has allowed me to explore new ideas and perspectives, and gain a deeper understanding of myself and my place in the world.

Moreover, I have discovered that loneliness can spark creativity and innovation, leading me to new breakthroughs in my work and personal life.

Embracing loneliness has made me more resilient and self-sufficient. I have learned to find happiness within myself and not rely solely on others for my well-being.

So, while loneliness can be difficult and painful, it is also an opportunity for growth and self-discovery. By embracing it and exploring its depths, we can unlock new possibilities and achieve great things that we never thought possible.

Although there is transformative potential to loneliness, it's important to recognize that we still need the tools to address and overcome it. So, let's take the first step towards finding those tools.

2. LEARNING TO LOVE YOURSELF
Building Self-Love and Acceptance

"Love yourself first and everything else falls into line. You really have to love yourself to get anything done in this world." - Lucille Ball

In my opinion, we have one job to do in life, and that is to love ourselves.

I've realised that self-love is the foundation of all true connection and belonging. When we don't love and accept ourselves, we create a void that can't be filled by external connections or validation. We may have many friends, followers, or even romantic partners but, until we learn to love ourselves, we will always feel disconnected and alone.

If we pause and reflect, we can analyse any situation and recognize how we are demonstrating self-love in that particular moment.

When we love ourselves, we're more likely to make choices that are good for us, both physically and mentally. We're more likely to set boundaries with others and stand up for ourselves when we need to. We're more likely to prioritize self-care and take time to do things that bring us joy and fulfilment.

Loving ourselves isn't always easy. It's something we have to learn to do, and it takes practice. There will be times when we don't feel great about ourselves, when we feel like we're not enough, when we're struggling with difficult circumstances. But even in those moments, we can choose to be kind to ourselves, to treat ourselves with compassion and understanding, and to remind ourselves that we're doing the best we can.

When I encounter a challenging situation, I find

it so helpful to ask myself, "How am I showing love to myself in this moment?"

Whether we're dealing with a challenging work situation, a difficult relationship, or just the ups and downs of daily life, taking a moment to check in with ourselves and assessing how we're treating ourselves can be a powerful way to cultivate self-awareness and self-compassion.

Of course, there will be times when it can feel almost impossible to find anything to be grateful for. But, even in those moments, there's always something we can appreciate. Even if it's just the fact that we're still here, still breathing, still alive. And when we can find even the tiniest bit of gratitude, it can help shift our perspective and remind us that there is always hope for a better tomorrow.

Learning to love ourselves isn't always easy but, I honestly believe, that it's the most important work we can do in this life. And when we can love ourselves, flaws and all, we open ourselves up to a world of possibility, and joy, that we might never have known otherwise.

After my second divorce, I needed to find a

new place to live. I didn't have a lot of money, so the only affordable option was an apartment above a café on the main street in town.

The apartment had a cold and uninviting feel to it. The stove and oven were so old I didn't know how I was going to cook any decent meals, and I had to climb several flights of stairs every day. To make matters worse, on my first night there, while in bed, I almost cried when I heard the couple next door having sex. I felt so overwhelmed and asked myself, "Where have I landed?"

I remember feeling very sorry for myself, thinking that things couldn't possibly get worse. I was emotionally drained, full of self-doubt and insecurity, embarrassed about a second marriage ending, and alone.

But, I also remember, at the same time feeling extremely grateful to be out of the bad situation I was in. Upon reflection, although I had a long way to go, I recognize that some level of self-love and value must have been present within me to have had the courage to leave my marriage, and to believe that I deserved better in life.

Finally, I came to the conclusion that I had to change my mind-set, and to make the best out of my current situation, because nobody else could do it for me.

Consequently, as a result of this shift, a sense of contentment and gratitude came over me. I became grateful for having a roof over my head, and a place to call home. I also reassured myself that change is inevitable, and that someday I would be in a better place, both emotionally and physically.

I decided to make the apartment as comfortable as possible. The first thing I did was to move my bed to the opposite wall. I bought a rug for the sitting room floor, cushions and throws for the worn sofas, and lamps and candles to create a nice atmosphere.

I lived in that apartment for one full year, and it turned out to be one of the most exceptional years of my life. During my stay there, I discovered so much about myself, and embarked on a journey of personal growth.

In addition, much to my surprise, I cooked some of the most amazing meals on that old stove and, thankfully, I never again heard any unwanted sounds coming from the apartment next door.

When we accept what is, love ourselves, and be grateful for what we have in the moment, in my opinion, is the secret to happiness.

I believe that this is a powerful perspective that can transform the way we approach life. When we prioritize self-love, we create a foundation of resilience and compassion that allows us to weather any storm with greater ease and grace.

To love ourselves in all situations means to treat ourselves with kindness, respect, and understanding, regardless of what is happening around us. It means acknowledging our strengths and weaknesses, embracing our flaws and imperfections, and forgiving ourselves for our mistakes.

When we face difficult situations, like loneliness, it can be easy to fall into self-criticism or self-judgment. However, when we approach ourselves with love and compassion, we can find the inner strength to over-come challenges and emerge stronger and more resilient.

In this book, we will explore many ways in which we can demonstrate self-love.

3. OVERCOMING NEGATIVE SELF-TALK
How to Silence your Inner Critic

I

"The voice in the head has a life of its own. Most people are at the mercy of that voice; they are possessed by thought, by the mind. And since the mind is conditioned by the past, you are then forced to re-enact the past again and again." - Eckhart Tolle

Our thoughts, like our breath, are constantly moving and changing, and it is normal for us to experience both positive and negative thoughts.

But, have you ever noticed that it's easier to focus on the bad things that happen to us rather than the good? Well, there's actually a scientific explanation for this. Researchers have found that humans have a natural tendency towards negative thinking, which is known as the "negativity bias".

The negativity bias means that negative events and experiences have a greater impact on our mental state and behaviour than positive ones. This is because our brains have evolved to prioritize information that could potentially harm us, such as danger or negative feedback, over information that is neutral or positive.

Another reason why we tend to have negative thoughts is because of our past experiences. Negative experiences can leave a stronger impression on our minds than positive experiences, which can lead us to remember and dwell on them more.

While negative thinking can be harmful to our mental health, it's important to remember that it's a natural and normal aspect of being human.

But, by becoming more aware of our negative thoughts, and practicing positive thinking, we can learn to balance our thoughts and cultivate a more positive outlook on life.

Eckhart Tolle, author of The Power of Now, is a well-known spiritual teacher who, in his early years, experienced negative self-talk and overwhelming feelings of self-doubt. He would spend hours ruminating on his past mistakes and worrying about the future, leading him to feel disconnected and unable to find peace within himself. This led to intense feelings of anxiety and depression.

However, one night when Eckhart Tolle was in his late 20s, he had a powerful spiritual experience. He became aware of the present moment, and recognized that all his worries and anxieties were rooted in either past regrets or future fears that were outside of his control.

Here is an excerpt from The Power of Now where the author tells us about the importance of living in the present moment: *"Nothing ever happened in the past that can prevent you from being present now; and if the past cannot prevent you from being present now, what power does it have? The only power there is, is the power you give to the past when you carry it with you in your mind. Do you have problems now? Do you have a disease, a worry, or a negative thought? Those are problems that you can deal with now. The past has no power to solve them, and you cannot solve them in the future. The only time you can deal with them is now. Presence is the key to freedom, so you must learn to live fully in the present moment, where life is happening."*

The tendency towards negative thinking can also be linked to feelings of loneliness. Research has shown that lonely people are more likely to have negative thoughts and interpret social situations in a negative way.

For example, when you're feeling lonely, it's easy to misinterpret social situations. A seemingly normal interaction with someone might make you think that they don't like you or are purposely avoiding you. This negative thinking can spiral out of control and make you feel even more isolated, creating a vicious cycle that's hard to break.

Moreover, the negativity bias can also play a role in how lonely individuals perceive their own self-worth. People who are lonely may be more likely to focus on their shortcomings and negative qualities, leading to feelings of inadequacy and low self-esteem.

To break this cycle, it is important to develop awareness of our thoughts and the impact they have on us. This can involve practicing mindfulness and learning to observe our thoughts without judgment or attachment. By recognizing that negative thoughts are a natural part of being human, and learning to relate to them in a more mindful and compassionate way, we can reduce their power over us and experience greater peace and well-being in our lives.

If we're constantly telling ourselves negative things, we're more likely to believe them and act in ways that reinforce our negative beliefs. This can lead to a self-fulfilling prophecy where we withdraw from social situations or avoid forming new relationships altogether.

The good news is that negative self-talk can be challenged and overcome.

There are several strategies that can help us identify and challenge our negative self-talk, they are **Mindfulness and Meditation, Cognitive Restructuring, and Self-Compassion.** I will be discussing these in the following chapters.

4. MINDFULNESS AND MEDITATION
The Power of the Present Moment

"The mind is everything. What you think you become". – Buddha

As discussed in the previous chapter, when we're feeling lonely, it can be all too easy to get caught up in negative thoughts and emotions, which only perpetuate our feelings of isolation. However, practicing mindfulness and meditation can help break this cycle by allowing us to be more present in the moment and cultivate a sense of inner peace and self-awareness.

Mindfulness and Meditation are related practices, but they are not exactly the same thing.

Mindfulness is a state of awareness in which we are fully present and engaged in the current moment, without judgment or distraction. It involves paying attention to our thoughts, feelings, bodily sensations, and surroundings in a non-judgmental way, and accepting them for what they are. It can be practiced at any time, anywhere, and in any situation.

Mindfulness can be incredibly beneficial for managing negative thinking. When we practice mindfulness, we learn to observe our thoughts without judgement, which can help us to recognize negative thinking patterns and prevent them from spiralling out of control.

Through mindfulness, we become more aware of our thoughts and emotions, and we learn to respond to them in a more balanced and compassionate way. This can help us to break free from negative thinking patterns and replace them with positive ones.

There are plenty of ways to practice mindfulness, so you can find what works best for you. The important thing is to approach each activity with an open mind and curiosity, and gently guide your attention back to the present moment when your mind starts to wander.

Here are some examples of mindfulness practices you can try:

- *Mindful breathing:* Take a few minutes to focus on your breath. Notice the sensation of air moving in and out of your nose and mouth. If your mind wanders, gently bring your focus back to your breath.

- *Body scan*: Lie down or sit comfortably and bring your attention to each part of your body, starting with your toes and working your way up. Notice any sensations without judgment.

- *Mindful walking*: Take a walk and focus on the sensation of your feet touching the ground. Notice the sights, sounds, and smells around you.

- *Mindful eating*: Slow down and savour each bite of your food. Notice the flavours and textures, and pay attention to the sensation of chewing and swallowing.

- *Mindful listening*: Practice active listening by fully engaging with the person who is speaking to you, and focusing on their words without distraction. Or Listen to music, or nature sounds, and focus on the different layers of sound. Notice how each sound makes you feel.

Remember, these are just a few examples. We can be mindful in any activity by bringing our attention fully to the present moment and noticing our thoughts and feelings without judgment.

Meditation, on the other hand, is a more formal practice that involves training the mind to focus and concentrate. It often involves sitting or lying down in a quiet place, closing your eyes, and focusing your attention on a specific object or mantra. Meditation can help to calm the mind, reduce stress and anxiety, and improve overall well-being.

While mindfulness can be practiced in many different ways, including meditation, meditation is just one of many techniques used to cultivate mindfulness. Mindfulness can be practiced through activities such as walking, eating, or even cleaning, whereas meditation is typically a more formal and structured practice.

Here are some meditation practices for you to try:

- *Guided meditation*: Maybe you could find a meditation group to join in your area, or you can listen to a guided meditation which can be found online or through various meditation apps. A guide will talk you through the process and help you stay focused.

- *Loving-kindness meditation*: Sit in a comfortable position and focus on sending love and kindness to yourself and others. You can repeat phrases such as "may I be happy," "may I be healthy," "may I be peaceful," and so on. Then, extend these phrases to loved ones, acquaintances, and even those you have difficulty with.

- *Visualization meditation*: This involves imagining a peaceful scene or a positive outcome for a situation in your life. You can use all your senses to create a vivid mental image.

- *Mantra meditation*: This involves repeating a word or phrase, either silently or out loud, to help focus your attention and quiet your mind. You can use a traditional mantra like "Om" or choose your own word or phrase that resonates with you.

In short, mindfulness is a state of being, while meditation is a specific technique that can help you achieve that state.

Overall, Mindfulness and Meditation are powerful tools that can help us overcome negative self-talk. However, by practicing mindfulness and meditation, we can learn to recognize negative self-talk patterns and interrupt them before they spiral out of control.

Personally when I discovered mindfulness and meditation, it changed everything.

With continued practice, I find that it helps me

to develop a more positive and compassionate outlook on life. It allows me to cultivate a sense of inner peace and contentment that helps me to feel more connected to others and less alone.

Personally, practicing mindfulness and meditation have been one of the most powerful tools in my journey towards overcoming loneliness and negative thinking. They have helped me to cultivate a more positive and compassionate mind-set, and have given me the tools to overcome the negative thought patterns that were holding me back.

5. COGNITIVE RESTRUCTURING
Rewiring your Brain for Positive Change

"The greatest discovery of my generation is that a human being can alter his life by altering his attitudes." – William James

Have you ever found yourself stuck in negative thought patterns that just make you feel worse and worse? Like when you're feeling lonely and you start thinking "I'm always going to be alone" or "Nobody wants to hang out with me." As we're learning, these thoughts seem like they're based in reality, but they're actually just a product of our own minds. This is where

Cognitive Restructuring comes in. It's a technique that will help you break free from those negative thoughts and replace them with more positive and realistic ones.

So how does Cognitive Restructuring work? First, you need to become aware of your negative thought patterns. This means paying attention to your thoughts and emotions and identifying when you feel anxious, depressed, or upset.

Become mindful of your inner dialogue and emotional reactions, and notice your thoughts as they come and go, without judgment or analysis.

To begin this process, you can try taking a few deep breaths and focusing your attention on the present moment. This can help you become more aware of your thoughts and emotions.

Once you have become more mindful of your thoughts, you can begin to identify any negative patterns. For example, you might notice that you tend to catastrophize situations or focus on the worst-case scenario. You might also notice that you have certain negative beliefs about yourself or others, such as "I'm not good enough" or "People always let me down." or "I'll never have company".

Once you have identified these negative thought patterns, you can begin to challenge them.

You might try looking for evidence that contradicts your negative thoughts. You might ask yourself questions like "Is this thought true?" or "What evidence do I have to support this thought?"

For example, if you have the thought, "I'm not good enough", you could look for evidence of times when you have succeeded or received positive feedback. Or, if you have the thought "I am always alone", you could look for evidence of times when you've had positive social experiences, and have friends who care about you.

Once you've challenged these negative thoughts, it's time to replace them with more positive and realistic ones. This means finding a way to reframe your thinking in a way that feels true and helpful.

For example, if you have the thought, "I'm not

good enough", try thinking "I am capable and competent. I have achieved success in the past and can do it again". Or, instead of thinking "I'm always going to be alone," try thinking "I have people who care about me and I can take steps to connect with others."

Here are some more examples:

- *"Nobody likes me."*
  "I have friends and family who do care about me. "I love and approve of myself".

- *"I always mess things up."*
  "I don't always mess things up."
  "I am not perfect, but I can learn from my mistakes and improve in the future."

- *"I'm never going to get over this."*
  "Healing takes time, but I am taking steps to move forward and make progress."

- *"I'm a failure."*
  "I am capable of success".
  "I have had setbacks, but I am not defined by them. I can learn from them and use them as motivation to succeed."

As you practice paying attention to your thoughts, you may begin to notice certain patterns or situations that trigger negative thinking. These triggers could be things like stress at work, being alone for too long, or even just feeling hungry or tired.

Once you recognize what triggers your negative thoughts, you can take steps to manage or avoid them in the future. This can include things like taking breaks during a stressful workday, or making plans to spend time with friends when you know you'll be alone. By addressing your triggers, you can prevent negative thoughts from overwhelming you and maintain a more positive outlook.

To sum up, paying attention to your thoughts means being aware of what's going on in your head and how it makes you feel. You have to recognize when you're having negative thoughts and figure out why you're having them. Then, you need to ask yourself questions and look for evidence to challenge those thoughts. It takes practice but, by doing this, it can help you to rewire your thinking and, as a result, will help you to think more positively and realistically, and be more in control of your emotions. This can lead to a greater sense of well-being, improved mood, and increased social connectedness *and,* surprisingly, you might find evidence that you actually *do* have friends or family members who care about you, and you *have* had positive social experiences in the past. You might also come to the conclusion that your thoughts do not define who you are, or define your future.

To further help you with this topic I would like to recommend two brilliant authors, *Byron Katie* and *Louise Hay.*

Byron Katie

If you haven't already discovered her teachings, I highly recommend *"THE WORK" by Byron Katie,* which is a process of inquiry that involves questioning our thoughts and beliefs that cause suffering in our lives. Katie offers a unique approach to confronting and challenging the harmful effects of negative self-talk and assumptions about ourselves and others.

In the words of Byron Katie.......*"I discovered that when I believed my thoughts I suffered, but when I didn't believe them I didn't suffer, and that this is true for every human being. Freedom is as simple as that. I found that suffering is optional. I found a joy within me that has never disappeared, not for a single moment. The joy is in everyone, always. And I invite you not to believe me. I invite you to test it for yourself."*

I highly recommend the following books:

"Loving What Is", "A Mind at Home with Itself, and *"I Need Your Love – Is That True"*

In *"Loving What Is,"* Byron Katie introduces her powerful method of self-inquiry, "The Work". This book offers practical guidance on how to identify and question our limiting beliefs, and provides tools for developing greater self-awareness, self-acceptance, and inner peace.

In *"A Mind at Home with Itself,"* Katie expands upon her teachings by exploring the nature of the mind and consciousness. She draws upon her own personal experiences and insights to offer a deeper understanding of how the mind works, and provides tools and practices for cultivating greater clarity, presence, and awareness.

In *"I Need Your Love - Is That True?"* Katie explores the often painful and limiting beliefs we hold around love and relationships. In the book, Katie offers a radical approach to transforming our relationships by questioning the beliefs and assumptions we hold about love, and developing a greater sense of self-love and acceptance.

You can also find Byron Katie on YouTube where you will see her in action challenging people's beliefs, and watch as she helps them question their own thinking.

Louise Hay

"You Can Heal Your Life" by Louise Hay offers powerful insights and practical techniques that can help you transform your thoughts and beliefs to overcome challenges and achieve greater happiness.

Louise Hay's journey to healing, through changing her thoughts, began with her own personal struggles and challenges. After experiencing childhood abuse and a difficult marriage, she began to develop a deep interest in spirituality and self-help.

Through her studies and personal experiences, she came to believe that our thoughts and beliefs have a profound impact on our emotional and physical health. She began to explore different techniques for changing negative or irrational thought patterns, such as affirmations and visualization.

As Louise Hay began to practice these techniques, she found that they had a transformative effect on her life. By changing her thoughts and beliefs, she was able to overcome her emotional wounds and physical ailments, and develop a deep sense of self-love and self-compassion, which allowed her to move forward in her life with greater happiness and fulfilment.

Her story is a powerful testament to the transformative power of our beliefs and the importance of self-love and self-care in achieving greater emotional and physical wellbeing.

Below are some positive affirmations by Louise Hay:

"I am capable of achieving anything I set my mind to."

"I choose to fill my life with positivity and love."

"I trust that everything is happening for my highest good."

"I am worthy of love and respect, just as I am."

My personal favourites are: *"Every day, in every way, my life gets better and better"*, and *"I release all negative thoughts and emotions and embrace peace and happiness."*

When we repeat affirmations to ourselves, we are sending positive messages to our subconscious mind.

Interestingly, did you know that the subconscious mind is unable to distinguish between the truth and a lie? This means that the subconscious processes information without questioning its validity or accuracy. As a result, when we repeatedly tell ourselves something, even if it isn't entirely true, our subconscious mind will start to believe it, and it eventually becomes our reality.

So, I encourage you to make positive affirmations a daily habit, if you haven't already. I personally believe that they are miracle workers which have made a significant impact on my life.

By intentionally choosing positive and uplifting statements, and repeating them regularly, we start to shift our mind-set towards positivity and self-empowerment.

6. SELF-COMPASSION
Learning to Treat Yourself with Kindness

"Self-compassion is not a luxury, it is a necessity. In order to treat others with kindness and compassion, we must learn to treat ourselves that way first." – Kristin Neff

Self-compassion is all about treating ourselves with kindness and understanding, especially during times when we're feeling difficult emotions. This can mean taking care of ourselves through self-care activities like getting enough rest, exercise, and nutritious food, surrounding ourselves with positive people, and doing things that make us happy and proud of ourselves. By practicing self-compassion, we learn to treat ourselves with the same level of care and compassion that we would offer to our loved ones during tough times.

Self-care:
- Take a relaxing bath or shower with your favourite scented soap.
- Treat yourself to a massage, facial, or other pampering spa treatment.
- Spend time in nature, whether it's going for a walk in the park, hiking in the mountains, or relaxing by the beach.
- Read a book or watch a movie that you've been wanting to see for a while.
- Take a nap or get a full night's sleep.
- Cook a healthy and nutritious meal for yourself.
- Listen to calming music or a guided meditation.
- Engage in a creative hobby, such as painting, drawing, or writing.
- Exercise or practice yoga to get your body moving and release endorphins.
- Spend time with loved ones who make you feel supported and uplifted.

It's important to remember that self-care looks different for everyone, and there is no one "right" way to do it. Some people may enjoy taking a long bath or practicing yoga, while others may prefer going for a run or reading a book. Whatever it is that brings you joy and relaxation, make it a priority in your life.

Remember that self-care is not selfish or indulgent, but rather a necessary part of maintaining good mental and emotional health. So, take some time to reflect on what activities or practices feel right for you and make them a regular part of your self-care routine.

Exercise
Regular exercise is important for our well-being because it helps improve physical and mental health, reduces stress, increases energy, and promotes better sleep.

You don't have to engage in intense exercise to reap the benefits. Even low-intensity activities such as walking, yoga, or gardening can have a positive impact on our physical and mental health. The key is to find activities that you enjoy and that you can incorporate into your daily routine.

Nutritious food
I have noticed that the food I eat really affects how I'm feeling. Did you know that what we eat can actually have a big impact on our mental health?

Eating a healthy, balanced diet that includes lots of fruits, vegetables, whole grains, lean proteins, and healthy fats can actually help improve our mood, cognitive function, and overall well-being.

Here's the science bit: Certain nutrients, like omega-3 fatty acids, vitamin B12, and folate, help our body produce chemicals called neurotransmitters that help regulate our mood, like serotonin, dopamine, and norepinephrine. And by eating foods that are rich in these nutrients, we can actually promote the production of these feel-good chemicals in our brain.

Furthermore, eating a healthy diet can also help reduce inflammation in our body, which has been linked to mental health issues like depression and anxiety. Plus, it can help keep our blood sugar levels stable, which can lead to better energy and mood throughout the day.

Things like vitamin D, iron, and magnesium are crucial for our brain and body to function at their best, and you can get them by eating a varied and balanced diet.

So, if you want to take care of your mental health, start by paying attention to what you are eating. By choosing nutrient-rich foods and avoiding processed and sugary foods, you can help your brain and body function at their best and improve your overall well-being.

Surround yourself with positive people: Surrounding yourself with positive people is crucial for your mental and emotional well-being. Being around negative people can bring you down and make it difficult to maintain a positive outlook on life.

It's not about the quantity of friends, but the quality of your relationships. If you have one good friend who supports you, encourages you, and brings positivity into your life, that's worth more than a large group of negative people.

Having positive people in your life can also help boost your self-esteem, provide emotional support during tough times, and improve your overall mood. Positive people can also inspire and motivate you to achieve your goals and pursue your passions.

So, make an effort to surround yourself with positive people, even if it's just one friend. Seek out people who uplift you and bring positivity into your life. By doing so, you'll improve your mental and emotional well-being and create a happier, more fulfilling life.

Practice self-forgiveness: It's important to recognize that we all make mistakes and that's okay. Instead of beating ourselves up over our past mistakes, we should focus on learning from them and using them as opportunities for growth.

For me, practicing self-forgiveness has been a journey. I used to be very hard on myself for my mistakes and would often dwell on them for days, weeks, or even months. But I've learnt that this kind of negative self-talk only makes things worse. Now, when I make a mistake, I try to remind myself that it's okay to be human and that everyone makes mistakes. I focus on what I can do to make things right and move forward.

One way to practice self-forgiveness is to write a letter to yourself, acknowledging the mistake you made and how it made you feel. Then, forgive yourself for the mistake and focus on what you can do to learn from it and grow as a person. Another way is to practice self-compassion, treating yourself with the same kindness and understanding you would offer a good friend.

Remember, practicing self-forgiveness is not about excusing our mistakes or avoiding responsibility. It's about acknowledging our mistakes, taking responsibility for them, and using them as opportunities for growth. By practicing self-forgiveness in a positive way, we can improve our self-esteem, reduce stress and anxiety, and create a more positive and fulfilling life.

In conclusion *please remember to*:

- Practice mindfulness and meditation.
- Reframe negative thoughts.
- Practice positive affirmations.
- Practice self-care.
- Eat nutritious food.
- Surround yourself with positive people.
- Practice self-forgiveness.

Practicing these strategies regularly can help you to cultivate greater self-compassion and kindness towards yourself, leading to improved mental health and wellbeing.

Remember, it's important to be patient with yourself and to celebrate small victories along the way.

7. NURTURING YOUR INNER CHILD
Reconnecting with that Beautiful Part of Yourself

"Healing the inner child means that you learn to parent yourself with unlimited compassion and tenderness." - Thich Nhat Hanh

Having an inner child refers to the idea that we all have a part of ourselves that retains some of the innocence, playfulness, and curiosity of our childhood.

This inner child represents the carefree and uninhibited version of ourselves that we may have lost touch with as we grew older and took on more responsibilities and expectations.

When we tap into our inner child, we may experience feelings of joy, creativity, and wonder. We may also be reminded of our passions, dreams, and values that we may have buried or ignored in our adulthood.

Nurturing our inner child can be a way to cultivate self-love, acceptance, and healing. It can help us to connect with our authentic selves and rediscover what brings us true happiness and fulfilment.

Our inner child represents the vulnerable and innocent part of ourselves that may have been neglected, hurt, or abandoned in our childhood. By reconnecting with this part of ourselves, we can gain a deeper understanding of our emotions, behaviours and beliefs.

Loving our inner child involves acknowledging the pain and wounds that we may have experienced in our past. It means providing ourselves with the care, compassion, and validation that we may have missed out on as children. We can do this by giving ourselves permission to feel our emotions, expressing them in healthy ways, and engaging in self-care activities that nurture our inner child's needs.

Connecting with our inner child can also help us to rediscover our sense of playfulness, creativity, and curiosity. We may find joy in activities that we enjoyed as children, such as drawing, dancing, or playing games. As we reconnect with our inner child, we may also become more aware of our limiting beliefs and negative self-talk. We can challenge these thoughts and replace them with more positive and empowering ones.

Ultimately, connecting and loving our inner child is a powerful tool for healing and personal transformation. It allows us to tap into our inner resources of resilience, compassion, and self-love, and to cultivate a deeper sense of authenticity and wholeness within ourselves.

My introduction to the concept of the "inner child" came from a meditation group I was part of. During one session, the teacher explained the meaning of having an inner child and guided us in accessing it. Although it felt a bit strange at first, I followed along.

The teacher encouraged us to listen to our

inner child and indulge in its desires. She guided us into a lovely meditation to help us connect with our younger self.

During the meditation, a delightful memory resurfaced within me. It was of my inner child who loved to spend hours drawing and colouring.

Afterwards, I bought a book of mandalas and spent many joyful hours colouring in its intricate designs. To my surprise, it instilled a deep sense of peace and contentment within me.

As I continued to nurture my inner child, I discovered that it was a powerful tool for self-love and healing. I started to pay attention to what my inner child needed and wanted, such as spending more time in nature or pursuing creative projects. By following through on these desires, I felt more fulfilled and happy.

Eventually, I enrolled in a fantastic art course near my home. Despite lacking drawing skills, I felt drawn to the creative environment and decided to give it a try. Over the next four years, I experienced a magical environment where I felt like I was playing every day. The other students, many of whom were better artists than me, were incredibly supportive and encouraging, and I felt at home among like-minded individuals.

Through this journey of nurturing my inner child, I gained a newfound love and appreciation for myself. I realized that by honouring my inner child's needs, I was able to access a deeper level of self-love and acceptance. It was a profound and transformative experience that continues to shape my life today.

Here are some ways for you to love and to connect with your inner child:

- **Acknowledge and validate your inner child's feelings:** When we experience emotional pain or distress, it can be helpful to imagine ourselves as children and think about what we would have needed at that time. *For example*, if we feel rejected or unloved, we might ask ourselves, "What would my inner child need to hear right now?" and then provide ourselves with kind, comforting words. By acknowledging our inner child's feelings and needs, we can learn to respond to ourselves with compassion and empathy.

- **Engage in activities that bring you joy:** Our inner child often holds the key to our passions and interests. By engaging in activities that bring us joy, such as playing an instrument, dancing, painting, or playing a sport, we can connect with our inner child and experience a sense of playfulness and creativity.

- **Practice self-care:** Taking care of our physical and emotional needs is an important way to love and nurture our inner child. This might include getting enough sleep, eating nourishing foods, practicing relaxation techniques like meditation or yoga, and seeking support from others when we need it.

- **Identify and heal childhood wounds**: Many of us have experienced childhood wounds or traumas that can impact our adult lives. By identifying these wounds and working to heal them, we can create a more loving and supportive relationship with our inner child. This might involve seeking therapy or counselling, journaling, or engaging in self-reflection and introspection.

- **Be playful and curious:** Our inner child thrives on playfulness and curiosity. By approaching life with a sense of wonder and openness, we can connect with our inner child and experience the joy and excitement of new experiences.

"Homecoming: Reclaiming and Championing your Inner Child" by John Bradshaw, is a great read for anyone looking to deepen their self-awareness and feel more whole.

This book guides us on a journey to reconnect with our inner child and heal from past traumas. It has practical tips and exercises to identify emotional wounds from our childhood and overcome any emotional barriers that are holding us back.

<u>Below is a meditation to help you connect with your Inner Child:</u>

Find a quiet and comfortable place where you won't be disturbed for a few minutes.

Sit or lie down in a comfortable position, close your eyes, and take a few deep breaths to relax your body.

Imagine a warm and loving light surrounding you, filling you with warmth and security.

Picture yourself standing in front of a door, visualize yourself opening the door and stepping inside.

As you walk through the door, allow yourself to be curious and open to whatever you encounter.

Look for a place where you feel safe and comfortable, like a beautiful garden or a cosy room. Once you find this place, sit down and make yourself comfortable.

Imagine your inner child standing in front of you, waiting to connect with you. See your child self and observe their appearance and behaviour.

Greet your inner child with warmth and compassion, and tell them that you are here to connect with them.

Ask your inner child what they need from you. Listen carefully to their response, and offer them love and understanding.

Spend some time connecting with your inner child, offering them the love and support they need to heal and thrive.

When you are ready, gently say goodbye to your inner child, knowing that you can return to this place anytime to connect with them again.

When you nurture your inner child, you will embark on a transformative journey that can lead to miraculous changes. You will begin to live a more authentic and joyful life, and create a meaningful existence for yourself.

8. CULTIVATING POSITIVE RELATIONSHIPS
How to connect with others

"The most basic and powerful way to connect to another person is to listen. Just listen. Perhaps the most important thing we ever give each other is our attention." - Rachel Naomi Remen.

As you work towards overcoming loneliness, building positive relationships with others is another crucial piece of the puzzle.

By cultivating strong and healthy connections with people around you, you can enhance your overall sense of well-being and help combat feelings of isolation.

In this chapter, we'll explore the significance of positive relationships and why they matter so much. Along with providing some practical advice on how to connect with others and build healthy, strong relationships that stand the test of time.

Having positive relationships with others can benefit us in so many ways. For one, it can give us a sense of belonging and community. When we feel connected to others, we're more likely to feel supported, valued, and understood.

Positive relationships can also help us to reduce stress and improve our mental health. When we have people in our lives who we can turn to for support and comfort, we're better equipped to deal with the challenges that come our way.

So how do we go about building positive relationships? Let's explore this in further detail.

Connect with others

If you're looking to expand your social circle and form meaningful relationships, it's important to step out of your comfort zone and connect with others. One way to do this is by reaching out to someone from your past, such as an old friend. You can send them a message or give them a call to catch up and see how they're doing. This can be a great way to rekindle a friendship and bring some joy to both of your lives.

Another effective approach to connecting with people is to join a club or group that aligns with your interests. Participating in clubs and organizations can help reduce feelings of loneliness by providing opportunities for social interaction and community involvement. For instance, joining a book club can help you meet new people who share your love of reading. You can discuss your thoughts and opinions on various books and gain insights into different perspectives.

Joining a volunteer group is also a great way to give back to your community and make a positive impact on the lives of others. You can meet like-minded individuals who share your passion for helping others and potentially form lasting connections. Additionally, participating in a fitness class, like yoga or Pilates, not only provides the physical benefits of exercise but also allows you to connect with others who are working towards similar goals. This can be a great way to make new friends and stay motivated.

Finally, joining a social club, such as a hiking club or a wine-tasting club, is a fun way to meet new people and explore new activities. You can bond over your shared interests and build lasting relationships. Whatever approach you choose, remember that building meaningful relationships takes time and effort. Be patient and keep an open mind, and you're sure to meet new people and form connections that enrich your life.

In case you haven't heard of Meetup.com, it is a website that connects people with similar interests in their local area. Here, you can search for groups based on your hobbies, profession, or any other interest, and attend events and gatherings with like-minded people.

When I first learned about Meetup.com, I was absolutely blown away. The story behind its creation is so inspiring: founder Scott Heiferman saw the way his community came together after the tragedy of 9/11, and wanted to use the internet to help bring people together in real life. He saw an opportunity to connect individuals with shared interests, whether that was cooking, photography, hiking, or anything else.

What I find most amazing about Meetup.com is its power to combat loneliness and isolation. By connecting with others who share our passions and hobbies, we can form a sense of community that might otherwise be lacking in our lives. It's a great example of how technology can be used to bridge the gap between the digital and physical worlds, and help people forge meaningful connections.

I myself am a member of Meetup.com, and my first experience with the platform was joining a group of women, who were either divorced or separated, who went on various outings together. The first outing I attended was to an Italian restaurant in my town in Ireland. Although I felt a bit nervous, I took a chance and decided to go.

Looking back, I am grateful that I did because the women I met were so nice, and we had a fantastic time getting to know each other. I recall leaving the event feeling more optimistic and hopeful than I had in a long time.

That one decision to attend a Meetup event had a huge impact on my life. It helped me break out of my shell and introduced me to a community of like-minded women who truly understood what I was going through. I was so thankful for the opportunity to connect with others and build lasting relationships.

Having empathy

If we want to have good relationships with others, it's important for us to be able to understand and share their feelings. This is called empathy, and it helps us connect with others, build trust, and communicate effectively.

Empathy is the ability to understand and share the feelings of another person. It is a significant contributor to developing and nurturing positive connections.

There are three main types of empathy: *Cognitive Empathy, Emotional Empathy, and Compassionate Empathy.*

Cognitive empathy is the ability to understand someone's perspective and emotions without necessarily feeling them yourself. It involves recognizing and acknowledging another person's feelings, but not necessarily experiencing them yourself.

Emotional empathy on the other hand, is the ability to actually feel the emotions of another person. This type of empathy involves an emotional connection to others, and can be particularly useful in situations where a person needs comfort or support.

Compassionate empathy involves not only feeling someone's emotions but also taking action to help them. This type of empathy involves a strong desire to alleviate another person's suffering and to take steps to improve their situation.

Did you know that empathy is something that can be learned and developed? There are a variety of techniques that you can use to cultivate empathy, such as: *Active Listening, Perspective-Taking, and Practicing Kindness and Compassion.*

Active listening is a technique that involves fully focusing on and engaging with the person who is speaking. It means paying attention not only to their words, but also their tone of voice, body language, and emotions.

For example, a friend is telling you about a difficult situation they're going through at work. Instead of just nodding along and waiting for your turn to speak, you can use active listening by making eye contact with your friend to show that you're fully present and engaged. Encourage them to keep talking by asking questions.

By actively listening in this way, you can show your friend that you care about them and their experiences, and create a deeper connection between the two of you.

Perspective-taking is when you try to put yourself in the other person's shoes and imagine how they might be feeling, instead of just offering advice or trying to cheer them up.

By listening attentively to their answers and trying to understand their perspective, you can show your friend that you care and are there to support them in a meaningful way.

By putting ourselves in other people's shoes and truly understanding their feelings and experiences, we can create deeper connections, and foster greater compassion and empathy towards others.

Practice kindness and compassion towards your friend to offer your support and understanding. Listen to them vent about their problems without judgment, offer words of encouragement and reassurance, or even help them out with practical tasks like running errands or cooking them a meal. By showing that you care and are there for them, you can help to ease their burden and strengthen your relationship with them.

Effective Communication:

As we know, communication is key to building positive relationships. But, if we're honest, sometimes we can forget the most important aspect of effective communication when we're in social situations.

When we're meeting new people, it's so easy to get caught up in trying to impress them or make a good impression. We might think about all the interesting things we can say, or the impressive stories we can share to make ourselves seem more exciting. While it's natural to want to showcase our best selves when meeting new people, approaching conversations with the intention of impressing others can often seem insincere.

So it's important to pause and remind ourselves of what really matters when it comes to effective communication. Instead of trying to get something from others, we should focus on bringing something to them. This means being genuinely interested in the people we're talking to and really listening to what they have to say.

When we think about it, when someone takes the time to really listen to us and show interest in what we have to say, we feel seen and valued. It's a powerful experience, and it's one that we can give to others simply by being present and engaged in our conversations.

Of course, effective communication is a two-way street. It's not just about listening to others, but also being willing to share ourselves when appropriate. By opening up and sharing our own thoughts, feelings, and experiences, we create a space for others to do the same.

So, let's keep this in mind the next time we find ourselves in the company of new people. It's not about impressing them or getting something from them. It's about being genuinely interested in them, listening to them, and sharing ourselves as well.

If you are not so great at small talk, or you feel shy around new people, a book I would recommend is *"The Fine Art of Small Talk"* by *Debra Fine*. This is a fun and practical guide to getting better at chatting with people. It's all about starting conversations, keeping them going, and making new friends by being chatty and friendly.

Debra Fine tells funny stories and gives examples of how to talk to people in a way that's interesting and engaging. She gives exercises and tips to help you practice what you learn, and reminds you to be interested the people around you.

While we are on the subject of cultivating positive relationships, I would like to discuss a topic close to my heart, which is the topic of starting a new romantic relationship as a way to prevent feelings of loneliness.

While a romantic relationship can be a source of joy and companionship, getting into a relationship solely to avoid feeling lonely can be very risky.

Certainly, it is possible to find a wonderful partner while experiencing loneliness. However, it's important to be cautious because there is a risk of settling for someone who may not be the best match for us in the long run.

When we are feeling lonely, we may be more likely to overlook red flags or compromise on our standards in order to alleviate our feelings of isolation. This can result in a relationship that lacks compatibility, mutual respect, and shared values, leading to conflicts and a lack of fulfilment in the long term. The real danger is you may be more likely to overlook red flags because you are so eager to avoid being alone.

If you enter into a relationship to avoid feeling lonely, you may end up developing an unhealthy attachment to your partner. This can lead to a situation where you become overly dependent on them for your emotional well-being, which can put a strain on the relationship. Also, you may be less likely to address issues that arise which can lead to resentment and further emotional isolation.

Moreover, when you replace loneliness with a romantic relationship you may miss out on opportunities for personal growth and exploration. You may miss out on pursuing interests and hobbies that can enrich your life and build your sense of self.

It's important to remember that while a romantic relationship can be a source of companionship and love, it is not a solution for alleviating feelings of loneliness.

I reflect on my own journey with entering into a relationship to escape pain and loneliness, and think to myself, if only I had known then what I know now.

Of course, we all do our very best with what we have at the time, but I wish I knew better.

Looking back, I realize that if only I had known the valuable lessons that could be gained from staying with my loneliness, I would have approached it with a very different mind-set.

If only I had understood that solitude can be an opportunity for personal growth and self-discovery, I would have seen it as a gift rather than a curse.

Instead of running away from it or trying to fill the void with distractions, I could have used the time to reflect on my values, beliefs, and aspirations, and to explore new interests and hobbies.

By facing my fears and insecurities, I could have become more resilient and self-reliant, and learned to appreciate my own company.

If I had truly believed that nothing stays the same forever, and that every experience, even the difficult ones, can teach us something, I might have found the courage and motivation to persevere.

If I had seen that loneliness was not my enemy, but my teacher, I would have welcomed it with open arms.

So it's essential for you to address the root cause of your loneliness so you can create a foundation for healthy relationships and a fulfilling life, regardless of whether you are in a romantic relationship or not.

Overall, by practicing the strategies in this chapter on *'Cultivating Positive Relationships'*, you can begin to build positive relationships and begin to overcome loneliness and have a more fulfilling and satisfying life. With the support of others, you can navigate the ups and downs of life, and find meaning, purpose, and happiness in your connections with others.

Of course, building positive relationships takes time and effort. It's important to be patient and persistent in your efforts to connect with others. You may not always hit it off with everyone you meet, but by putting yourself out there and making an effort to form connections, you will increase your chances of finding people who you really click with.

Finally, prioritize quality over quantity when it comes to your relationships. It's better to have a few close, supportive friends and family members than to have many shallow or unsatisfying connections. To build strong relationships, it's important to invest time and energy into nurturing these connections, whether through regular check-ins, shared activities, or other forms of support.

9. MANAGING SOCIAL ANXIETY
How to Overcome Fear and Isolation

"Your anxiety is not a curse. It is a gift. It's the alarm system that protects you from danger, it's the messenger that tells you when something needs to change, it's the energy that motivates you to take action." - Amy Clover

I just want to say that I can imagine how hard it must be for you to put yourself out there in social situations if you struggle with social anxiety. It can make you feel like you're the only one struggling while everyone else seems to be handling things with ease

Maybe you're anxious about meeting new people, going to parties, or even just being in a group setting. You may feel self-conscious, worry about being judged or criticized, or feel like you don't fit in.

But I want you to know that social anxiety is not a sign of weakness or inadequacy because it is a common struggle that many people experience. It is a natural response to situations that are unfamiliar or potentially threatening.

People with social anxiety may feel anxious or self-conscious in social situations, but this does not mean that they are weak or inadequate. It is simply a manifestation of their natural tendencies, meaning that feeling anxious or uncomfortable in social situations is a natural response for some people.

For example, some people may have a more introverted or shy personality, which can make socializing more challenging. Others may have had negative experiences in the past that have left them feeling anxious or self-conscious in social situations. In these cases, social anxiety is not a sign of weakness or inadequacy, but rather a reflection of the individual's unique tendencies and experiences.

By recognizing that social anxiety is a natural response, individuals can begin to understand and manage their anxiety in more effective ways.

Here are some tips that may help you overcome social anxiety:

- **Practice deep breathing:** When you feel anxious, your body's natural response is to breathe shallowly and rapidly. By practicing deep breathing, you can calm your body and reduce your anxiety. Take slow, deep breaths, inhaling through your nose and exhaling through your mouth.

- **Challenge negative thoughts:** Social anxiety can be fuelled by negative thoughts and beliefs about oneself and others. *(See Chapter 3)*

- **Gradual exposure:** Gradual exposure to social situations can help individuals with social anxiety build confidence and reduce their anxiety. Start by exposing yourself to situations that are mildly anxiety-provoking and gradually work your way up to more challenging situations.

Join a support group: Joining a support group

can be a great way to connect with others who are going through similar experiences. It can also provide a safe space to practice social skills and receive feedback and support.

Seek professional help: If social anxiety is interfering with your daily life, it may be beneficial to seek professional help from a therapist or counsellor. They can provide you with tools and strategies to manage your anxiety and improve your social skills.

It's important to remember that it takes courage to acknowledge and address social anxiety, and seeking help is a sign of strength and resilience

Below are two excerpts from the book "*The Shyness and Social Anxiety Workbook*" *by Martin M. Antony and Richard P. Swinson ,*

"Remember, shyness is not something you were born with and cannot change; it is a learned behaviour that can be unlearned. You can break the cycle of shyness and social anxiety by facing your fears and gradually building your confidence. As you begin to take risks and step outside your comfort zone, you will discover that you are capable of far more than you ever

imagined. You can learn to enjoy social situations, make new friends, and have fulfilling relationships. You can live a rich and rewarding life, free from the constraints of shyness and social anxiety."

"The goal is not to eliminate anxiety altogether; that's not possible, nor is it desirable. A certain amount of anxiety can be helpful in motivating you to prepare for social events, and it can help you perform at your best. The goal is to reduce the amount of anxiety that interferes with your ability to enjoy life and pursue your goals".

Remember that progress takes time, so be kind and loving to yourself along the way.

10. THE ART OF PRACTICING FORGIVENESS
How Letting Go can Improve your Life

"To forgive is to set a prisoner free and discover that the prisoner was you." - Lewis B. Smedes

An act of forgiveness is an expression of love and compassion towards ourselves and others. Through forgiveness, we can experience a sense of freedom, lightness, and openness to the abundance of blessings that surround us.

There is a saying *"Holding a grudge is like drinking poison and expecting the other person to die"*. This saying is so profound. When we hold onto anger, resentment, or bitterness towards someone who has wronged us, we are essentially poisoning ourselves with negative energy.

This negative energy can block the flow of positive energy and prevent us from experiencing the love, joy, and abundance that the universe has to offer. It can also create a sense of separation from others, including those we care about, which can contribute to feelings of loneliness.

From a spiritual perspective, forgiveness is a powerful tool for releasing this negative energy and opening ourselves up to the positive energy of the universe.

When we practice forgiveness, we are essentially releasing the other person from the hold they have on our energy, and allowing ourselves to move forward with greater peace. In this way, forgiveness is not just about letting go of anger or bitterness towards another person, but about reconnecting with the divine energy that flows through all of us, and experiencing a deeper sense of unity with others and the world around us.

What I have found to be so helpful when I feel I have been hurt by another, is to say - 'I am willing to offer this up for forgiveness'.

When we say the words *'I am willing to offer this up for forgiveness'* we create a space for ourselves to begin the journey of healing.

For me, the words, *'I am willing'*, help me to realise my willingness, and signifies that I am open to embarking on the journey of healing. By *'offering it up'* and surrendering it to the universe, rather than trying to force myself to forgive someone completely on my own, helps me to feel so much lighter and less burdened.

It's like we are saying 'I am willing to let go of this, and trust that something bigger than us will take care of the rest'.

So, if you're struggling to forgive someone who has hurt you, why not give it a try? Offer up your pain and hurt for forgiveness, and notice how it can help you feel lighter and more at peace as a result.

Also, when we hold onto grudges or refuse to forgive, we carry around negative emotions that can affect our mental and physical health.

These emotions can cause stress and anxiety.

But, it's important to note that forgiveness doesn't always mean forgetting what has happened or condoning someone's behaviour. Rather, it means acknowledging the hurt that has been caused, choosing to let go of negative emotions, and working towards a positive resolution. It's also important to remember that forgiveness is a process and may take time, especially if the hurt was severe.

Like us all, there have been times in my own life where I've been hurt by someone I trusted, and the thought of forgiving them seemed impossible. It felt like, by forgiving them, I would be letting them off the hook and condoning their behaviour. However, over time, I've learned that forgiveness is not about excusing someone's actions or forgetting what they did. It's about acknowledging the pain, and then making the choice to let go of the anger and resentment that's been holding me back.

It takes courage to forgive, and it's a journey that looks different for everyone. It isn't easy, but it's necessary for us to heal and move forward and to fully enjoy life and build positive relationships with others.

Since we're talking about forgiveness and people who have hurt us, it's worth mentioning how miscommunication can lead to hurt feelings.

Have you ever found yourself thinking that someone has wronged you, only to realize later on that it was just a miscommunication or a misunderstanding? It's a common experience, and it can happen to anyone. In fact, some of the greatest wars in history have been started as a result of miscommunication between nations or leaders. On a smaller scale, misunderstandings can cause rifts in personal relationships and lead to unnecessary conflicts.

Occasionally, we may hear something in the heat of the moment that we misinterpret or misunderstand. Alternatively, our own thoughts and internal dialogues can sometimes work against us, making us our own worst enemies. We jump to conclusions and assume the worst about the other person, even though they may not have intended to cause any harm.

It's important to remember that communication is key in any relationship, whether it's personal or professional. If you're feeling hurt or upset about something someone said or did, it's okay to express your feelings and have an open and honest conversation with them. They may not even realize that what they said or did was hurtful, and a simple explanation can clear up any confusion.

Of course, there are times when someone *does* intentionally cause harm, or act in a way that is unacceptable. In those situations, it's important to set boundaries and take care of yourself. However, in the case of a misunderstanding or miscommunication, it's worth giving the other person the benefit of the doubt and having a conversation to clear things up. You might be surprised at how much it can help to resolve the issue and strengthen your relationship.

In her book, "*The Gift of Change,* Marianne Williamson writes that there is a miracle waiting for us when we forgive.

She writes the following: "*Forgiveness is a miracle, a miracle that requires the letting go of judgment and the embracing of love. When we forgive, we release ourselves from the past and open ourselves up to the present. We let go of the hurt and pain that has been holding us back and we make room for healing and transformation.*

Forgiveness is not about condoning or excusing someone else's behaviour; it's about freeing ourselves from the burden of resentment and anger. It's about recognizing that we all make mistakes, and that we are all capable of both hurting and being hurt.

Forgiveness doesn't mean that we have to forget what has happened or pretend that everything is okay. It simply means that we choose to let go of our negative feelings and move forward with a heart full of love and compassion.

The miracle of forgiveness is that it sets us free. It frees us from the past, from our own negative thoughts and emotions, and from the cycle of hurt and pain. It allows us to connect more deeply with ourselves and with others, and it opens up a space for healing and growth.

So if you're struggling to forgive someone, remember that it's not about them; it's about you. It's about your own healing and your own journey towards love and wholeness. Trust in the miracle of forgiveness, and let it work its magic in your life."

So, by practicing forgiveness, we can break down the walls that we may have built around ourselves and open ourselves up to deeper connections with others. This can help alleviate feelings of loneliness by giving us a sense of belonging and connection to the world around us.

11. PERFECTIONISM
The Gift of being Perfectly Imperfect

"Perfection is not attainable, but if we chase perfection we can catch excellence." - Vince Lombardi

It's important to note that perfectionism is not the same as striving for excellence.

Here is what *Brené Brown* says about it in her book *"The Gifts of Imperfection"*.

"Perfectionism is not the same thing as striving to be your best. Perfectionism is the belief that if we live perfectly, look perfectly and act perfectly, we can avoid the pain of blame, judgment, and

shame. It's a shield. It's a twenty-ton shield that we lug around thinking it will protect us when, in fact, it's the thing that's really preventing us from flight. Perfect is driven by the fear of what other people will think. Imperfect is driven by a willingness to be vulnerable, to put ourselves out there even when there's no guarantee. Imperfect is about being real and connecting with others in a real way."

There's no one-size-fits-all answer to where perfectionism comes from, but some research suggests that experiences in childhood and adolescence may play a role. For me, although I had good parents and they did their very best, they were quite critical and over-controlling, I believe this contributed to my perfectionistic tendencies. I felt like I had to be perfect to earn their love and approval.

In addition, other experiences like academic or athletic pressure can also contribute to the development of perfectionism.

I also think that societal and cultural values play a role in perpetuating perfectionistic ideals. We're constantly bombarded with images and messages that tell us we need to be perfect to be happy and successful.

Of course, not everyone who experiences these things will become a perfectionist, and there are likely many other factors that contribute to the development of perfectionism. But for me, understanding where my perfectionism came from has helped me to be more self-aware and to work towards developing healthier habits and perspectives.

Here are some ways that perfectionism can be problematic:

Fear of Failure: Perfectionists often have an intense fear of failure and believe that anything less than perfect is unacceptable. This fear can cause anxiety and self-doubt, making it difficult to take risks or try new things.

Self-Criticism: Perfectionists are often highly self-critical, constantly finding fault in themselves and their work. This can lead to a negative self-image, low self-esteem, and feelings of shame and guilt.

Procrastination: Perfectionists may struggle with procrastination, as the fear of not being able to achieve their high standards can lead to avoidance or procrastination.

Burnout: Perfectionists often work long hours and put immense pressure on themselves to meet their high standards. This can lead to burnout, exhaustion, and even physical health problems.

Strained Relationships: Perfectionism can put a strain on personal and professional relationships, as the perfectionist may have unrealistic expectations of others and struggle to accept imperfections in themselves and others.

The Gift of being Perfectly Imperfect

Being perfectly imperfect is the idea that it's okay to be flawed, to make mistakes, and to not have everything in your life be "perfect". It's the understanding that perfection is an impossible and unrealistic standard to live up to.

It's essential for us to recognize, and remember, that we are all imperfect human beings with our own set of flaws and shortcomings. It's our imperfections that make us unique and special in our own way, and this is what makes us perfect just as we are.

Instead of constantly striving to meet societal or personal standards of perfection, we should learn to embrace our imperfections and use them as an opportunity to learn and grow. To accept ourselves for who we are, flaws and all.

Embrace your strengths and weaknesses, and recognize that both contribute to your unique identity and make you who you are.

This mind-set can lead to greater self-acceptance, self-compassion, and a more positive outlook on life. By embracing our imperfections and accepting ourselves for who we are, we can experience greater happiness, fulfilment, and authenticity in our lives.

To overcome perfectionism, it's important to practice self-compassion, challenge unrealistic expectations, and learn to accept imperfection.

This can involve setting more realistic goals, practicing self-care, and developing a growth mind-set that embraces failure as an opportunity for learning and growth. Seeking the help of a therapist can also be beneficial in overcoming perfectionism and building resilience.

Although loneliness can be a difficult feeling to embrace, it's important to remember that it too is a natural part of being human.

Just like our imperfections, it's what makes us unique and adds to our overall beauty and value as individuals. By embracing our loneliness and accepting it as a part of our journey, we can learn more about ourselves and what we truly need in life.

It's easy to fall into the trap of comparing ourselves to others or trying to meet unrealistic expectations of social interaction and popularity. But by embracing our individuality and accepting our loneliness, we can free ourselves from the pressures of conformity and societal expectations.

Just like our imperfections, our moments of loneliness can make us stand out from everyone else and allow us to contribute something valuable to the world. By accepting ourselves for who we are, flaws and all, we can live a happier and more fulfilling life.

So embrace your unique journey, celebrate your individuality, and know that you are perfect just as you are.

12. EMBRACING VULNERABILITY
How to open up and connect

"Vulnerability is the only authentic state. Being vulnerable means being open, for wounding, but also for pleasure. Being open to the wounds of life means also being open to the bounty and beauty." - Stephen Russell

Vulnerability is often seen as a negative trait, associated with weakness or being too emotional. However, it's important to recognize that vulnerability is a natural part of the human experience. It's not about being overly emotional or dramatic, but rather about being authentic and honest with ourselves and others.

When we are vulnerable, we allow ourselves to be seen and heard for who we truly are, and this can create opportunities for genuine connection and understanding. By being open and honest with others, we can build trust and deepen our relationships.

However, vulnerability can be difficult to embrace, particularly if we have experienced rejection or criticism in the past. It's important to recognize that vulnerability is a risk, but it's a risk worth taking in order to build meaningful connections with others.

I learned how to open up and be vulnerable through a good friend who was never afraid to share her thoughts and feelings. I remember being amazed by her courage to be so open and vulnerable with me.

Through her example, I learned how to do the same. She was never afraid to share her thoughts and feelings, and by doing so, she taught me so much about being open and honest. Seeing her vulnerability showed me that it's okay to let people in, and that being open is a sign of strength, not weakness. She created a safe space for me to be myself, and encouraged me to share my own thoughts and feelings. It was scary at first, but her support and understanding made it easier for me to open up.

Thanks to her, I've learned the importance of vulnerability in building strong relationships, and to be comfortable being honest with others.

<u>Here are some ways for you to find the courage to be vulnerable with others</u>:

- *<u>Sharing your feelings:</u>* It takes bravery to open up and share your innermost feelings with others. By allowing yourself to be vulnerable, you are taking a risk and putting yourself in a position of emotional openness and honesty.

- *<u>Admitting mistakes</u>*: It can be difficult to admit when you've made a mistake, but doing so requires vulnerability and bravery. By acknowledging your mistakes and taking responsibility for them, you demonstrate humility and a willingness to learn and grow.

- *<u>Asking for help</u>*: Asking for help can be a challenging and vulnerable experience.

It requires admitting that you don't have all the answers and need assistance from others. However, by reaching out for help, you are demonstrating bravery and a commitment to finding solutions and improving yourself.

- *Trusting others*: Trusting others can be a vulnerable experience, as it requires you to let down your guard and rely on others for support and understanding. By allowing yourself to trust others, you demonstrate a willingness to take risks in order to build deeper connections and relationships.

- *Sharing your story*: Sharing your personal story or experiences can be a vulnerable and courageous act. It requires you to open up about your vulnerabilities, struggles, and successes, and to allow others to see you for who you truly are. By sharing your story, you demonstrate courage and a commitment to authenticity and vulnerability.

- *Apologising*: Apologising takes guts and is a super vulnerable thing to do. You've got to have some serious courage and humility to say sorry when you mess up. People who can apologize are the ones who aren't afraid to admit their mistakes and take responsibility for their actions. They know that saying sorry doesn't make them weak, but actually shows that they're strong enough to own up to their faults. Those who can apologise also value their relationships and know that sometimes saying sorry is the key to keeping those connections strong. They're not afraid to work through conflicts and challenges, and are committed to making things right and moving forward.

In order to embrace vulnerability, it can be helpful to start small. This might involve sharing something personal with a trusted friend or family member, or even just acknowledging a feeling or thought that you might normally keep to yourself. By sharing this small truth, you'll begin to build trust and intimacy with others, and you'll learn that vulnerability doesn't always lead to negative outcomes.

Journaling your thoughts and feelings can be a powerful way to process emotions and develop greater self-awareness. Try setting aside a few minutes each day to write about your experiences of vulnerability. You might reflect on how you felt, what you learned, or what you could do differently next time. This practice can help you identify patterns in your thinking and behaviour and develop greater self-acceptance.

It's also important to practice self-compassion when it comes to vulnerability. This means recognizing that it's okay to feel scared or uncomfortable, and that you are not alone in these feelings.

By offering yourself kindness and understanding, you can build the courage to be vulnerable with others.

When it comes to vulnerability, it's important to be mindful of who you share your thoughts and feelings with. While vulnerability can lead to deeper connections with others, it's also important to protect yourself from those who might not have your best interests at heart.

One way to protect yourself is by setting healthy boundaries. This might involve being selective about who you share personal information with, or being clear about what you are and are not comfortable discussing. It can also mean saying no to situations or people that make you feel uncomfortable.

It's important to remember that you have the right to say no to any situation or person that does not feel right to you. This can be challenging, particularly if you are someone who struggles with people-pleasing, or has a history of being taken advantage of. However, setting boundaries is an important part of protecting yourself and your well-being.

In addition to setting boundaries, it can be helpful to pay attention to your intuition when it comes to vulnerability, it's important to trust that feeling and protect yourself from those who might not have your best interests at heart.

By being mindful of who you share your vulnerability with and being willing to set healthy boundaries, you can build deeper connections with others while also keeping yourself safe and protected.

Remember to:

- **Take time to get to know people:** It's important to take the time to get to know people before trusting them with personal information or investing too much time and energy into a relationship. It's okay to be cautious and to take things slow.

- **Trust your gut:** It's important to listen to your instincts when it comes to sharing your private thoughts with others. You need to be careful and choose people you know and trust. Your instincts are there for a reason, and they can help guide you to the right people to confide in. Learning to tune in and trust your instincts can help you make better decisions about who to share your deepest thoughts and feelings with.

- **Surround yourself with positive people:** Surrounding yourself with positive people is essential when it comes to vulnerability. When you open up and share your thoughts and feelings with others, you want to be sure that the people you're confiding in will support and uplift you. Being vulnerable can be scary, but having a strong support system can make all the difference. Positive people will not only listen to you, but they'll also encourage and inspire you to be your best self. They'll help you see the best in yourself, even when you're feeling down or discouraged. By surrounding yourself with positive people, you're giving yourself the gift of support, love, and encouragement, which can help you navigate vulnerability with greater ease and confidence.

- **Set boundaries:** When you're opening up to others, it's important to set clear boundaries to protect yourself from potentially harmful or toxic individuals. Knowing and communicating what you're comfortable with is key. Be firm but respectful when you establish these boundaries. This will not only help you feel safer and more in control, but it will also let others know what you're comfortable with and what your expectations are for the relationship.

- **Be assertive:** Being assertive is a big part of being vulnerable. When you're opening up and sharing your thoughts and feelings with others, you've got to be upfront about what you need and want from the relationship. Being assertive means standing up for yourself in a respectful way and being open to hearing what others have to say. It can be scary to open up, but if you don't communicate your needs clearly, you might end up feeling misunderstood or unsatisfied. When you're assertive, you're letting people know what you're looking for and what you won't put up with. This helps build trust and can lead to more meaningful connections. By being clear about what you need, you'll feel more respected and build stronger relationships.

By embracing vulnerability, you can open yourself up to deeper connections with others and overcome loneliness. It takes courage and strength to be vulnerable, but the rewards are well worth the risk.

13. THE MISPERCEPTION OF BEING STRONG
Breaking the Illusion

"Even the strongest people need someone to listen and understand." - Unknown

As I write this book, there's a topic that keeps coming to my mind, and that is the struggle faced by strong, independent individuals. I know this all too well, as I consider myself one of those people.

The misperception of being strong often arises from the assumption that someone who appears to be strong and independent has it all together and doesn't need help or support.

This can be a double-edged sword, as while it's great to be seen as capable and self-sufficient, it can also lead to feelings of isolation and the belief that one has to do everything on their own.

We often hear people say things like, "You're so strong," or "I don't know how you do it all." While these compliments can be nice to hear, they can also be a burden for those of us who consistently present ourselves as being strong and self-sufficient.

As humans, we all have moments of vulnerability and need for support. However, when we consistently present ourselves as strong and capable, others may assume that we are always fine and don't need help. This can create a self-fulfilling prophecy where the more we appear strong, the less likely others are to check on us or offer support.

Furthermore, the belief that we must be strong all the time can be exhausting and detrimental to our mental health. Constantly presenting ourselves as strong can prevent us from seeking help or sharing our struggles with others, leading to a sense of bottling up emotions and increased stress levels.

It's essential to remember that being strong doesn't mean we don't need support or can't ask for help. We all have moments of vulnerability, and it's important to acknowledge and share them with others. By doing so, we can break down the misconceptions that we're always okay and create stronger connections with the people around us.

Also, it's important to remember that everyone is fighting their own battles, and just because someone may appear to be doing well on the surface, it doesn't mean that they are not struggling inside. I've had to realise that other people too might have a tendency to hide their struggles and put on a brave face.

Therefore, it's essential to check in on the people in our lives, even those who seem to have it all together. We can't assume that they're doing okay just because they appear happy and successful. We need to take the time to ask how they're doing and listen to their response. Sometimes, even the simple act of reaching out and showing that we care can make a significant difference in someone's life.

When we take the initiative to check in on others, it can create a sense of community and support. We can all benefit from knowing that someone cares and is there to help us through difficult times. So, let's make an effort to check in on those around us, even if they seem strong and independent. We never know when a kind word or gesture could make all the difference.

In her memoir, "*The Art of Asking: How I Learned to Stop Worrying and Let People Help*" Amanda Palmer shares her personal journey of learning to ask for help and accept support from others. Despite her reputation as a strong and independent performer, Palmer writes about her struggles with asking for help and accepting vulnerability.

Through her own experiences and insights, as well as interviews with others, Palmer explores the power of connection, community, and vulnerability. She argues that asking for help is not a sign of weakness, but rather a powerful tool for building meaningful relationships and achieving success.

The book offers practical advice for overcoming fear and shame around asking for help, as well as insights into the ways in which vulnerability can transform our lives. It is a powerful and inspiring read for anyone looking to understand the importance of supporting even the strongest among us.

Here is an excerpt for this brilliant book: *"I had been brought up with the notion that asking for something meant you were weak, needy, and a burden on others. But it wasn't until I'd lived for years on the kindness of strangers that I began to realize the fallacy of this way of thinking. I'd always thought that by keeping my needs to myself, I was keeping myself safe from ridicule and rejection. But the opposite was true. By hiding my needs, I was hiding myself. And by denying the opportunity for others to give, I was denying them the chance to connect with me.*

Asking is, at its core, a collaboration. It's about recognizing that none of us can go it alone, and that we all have something to offer. When we ask for help or support, we're giving others the opportunity to be part of our journey, to share in our struggles and triumphs. And in turn, we're opening ourselves up to the support, wisdom, and love of those around us.

But asking can be scary. It means opening ourselves up to the possibility of rejection, disappointment, or even humiliation. It means admitting that we don't have all the answers, that we're not invincible, that we need others. But it's also the only way to truly connect with others, to build meaningful relationships, and to live a fulfilling life.

Learning to ask for help was one of the hardest things I've ever done. But it was also one of the most liberating. By opening myself up to the kindness and generosity of others, I was able to build a community of love and support that has sustained me through the hardest times. And I've come to realize that asking is not a weakness, but a strength. It's a recognition of our shared humanity, a celebration of our interdependence, and a powerful tool for building a more compassionate, connected world."

14. BREAKING THE HABIT OF SAYING 'NO'
Unlocking Opportunities

"Your habitual 'no' may be blocking the path to opportunities and growth. Break free from this pattern and embrace the power of 'yes."

– Unknown

Are you ever invited to go somewhere or do something, but your initial reaction is to say no? Maybe you're invited to a party or a social event, but the thought of going out and being around a lot of people just doesn't sound appealing.

This is a tricky subject, because prioritizing your own mental well-being and happiness may *require* you to say no at times and to disappoint others. Even if it means not attending an event you had previously committed to or going against your family's wishes. It's essential to prioritize your self-care and not compromise it just to seek validation from others. So, if saying no is what you need to do to take care of yourself, then it's okay to let someone down. Your self-love should always be a stronger force than the desire to be loved by others.

But, what I'm referring to here is that sometimes we decline invitations out of habit, rather than a genuine need to take care of ourselves.

I'll be honest, I'm a bit of a homebody. When I get an invitation to go somewhere or do something, my initial reaction is usually to say no. It's not that I don't like socializing or trying new things, but there's just something so comforting and familiar about being at home.

A Thanks to Loneliness

But lately, I've been realizing that declining invitations has become a habit with me. It's such a contradiction because I absolutely love getting an invitation. I want to be invited out and yet, at the same time, also want to stay at home.

If this is you too, I completely understand where you're coming from. On the one hand, we don't want to be lonely or miss out on fun experiences with friends or loved ones. On the other hand, staying at home can feel comfortable and safe, and we may even prefer the peace and quiet that comes with being alone.

It's true that sometimes we may only need an invitation to feel included and wanted by others, even if we don't necessarily feel the need to actually attend the event. Simply knowing that we were thought of and included can be enough to boost our self-esteem and sense of belonging. However, it's important to remember that saying no too often can have consequences. If we constantly decline invitations, we run the risk of being excluded from future events or activities. People may assume we're not interested or don't want to participate, and eventually they may stop inviting us altogether.

By saying yes, we open ourselves up to new experiences and possibilities that we may not have had otherwise. It's all about finding a balance between accepting invitations, and saying no when we genuinely don't feel up to it.

I have been trying to break the habit of my initial 'no' response, and to say 'yes' more often. As much as I love my home and the sense of peace it brings me, I know that I can't let that hold me back from experiencing life and building connections with others.

One thing that's been helpful for me is taking a moment to pause before responding to an invitation. Instead of immediately saying no, I give myself a little time to think about the opportunity and why I might be hesitant to try it. Sometimes it's because I'm nervous about meeting new people or trying something outside my comfort zone, but other times it's just because I'm feeling lazy or unmotivated. By taking a step back and acknowledging these feelings, I can make a more informed decision about whether or not to say yes to the invitation.

I try to focus on the positive aspects of the experience, like meeting new people or learning something new, instead of dwelling on the potential negatives. It's definitely a work in progress, but I'm starting to see the benefits of breaking my habit of saying no.

More importantly, have you ever found that, the invitation we initially wanted to decline ended up being the one that resulted in the most memorable experience.

In fact, some of my best memories stem from an event or outing that I was initially reluctant to attend. I ended up having a fabulous time, and met new friends that I would not have met otherwise.

So, the next time you receive an invitation that you're tempted to decline, try to remember that it could lead to a positive experience that you'll cherish for years to come. By saying yes, and stepping outside your comfort zone, you never know what exciting opportunities and connections you might make.

While we're on the subject of declining social invitations, I would like to discuss an interesting thought process that often occurs after we decline an invitation. *This process involves us <u>rationalizing</u> our decision. Psychologists refer to it as the decision-making dynamic of making a 'wrong' decision or a 'right' decision.*

I remember hearing about this dynamic years ago which I found it to be so interesting. And something I always think about before I decline an invitation, and the potential consequences that might occur in my mind as a result.

Let's say that a friend invites us to a social event, but we decline the invitation. The next step is where the process of rationalization and justification begins.

At first, we might experience feelings of guilt or regret for declining the invitation, and possibly letting down our friend. However, we may subsequently attempt to rationalize or justify our decision.

We may tell ourselves that we are too busy or too tired to attend. That the event wouldn't have been fun anyway, or that we're not in the mood to socialize.

Then, we may even go so far as to think negative thoughts about the person who invited us in order to further justify our decision. For example, we may tell ourselves that the person is always inviting us to boring events, or that they're not really good friends anyway.

By finding these justifications, we can alleviate our sense of guilt and convince ourselves that our decision not to attend was reasonable and justified.

Therefore, it's important to think twice before turning down an invite because your response can affect the other person. So, if you decline an invitation, just try to be honest with yourself, and take responsibility. Being honest with yourself and others is key to building genuine relationships and dealing with any negative feelings towards them. So, the next time, be mindful before declining that invitation!

But, please remember the importance of striking a balance, and to decline that invitation if it's appropriate to do so.

At the end of the day, it really is all about honouring and loving ourselves.

15. BUILDING A POSITIVE SELF-IDENTITY
Developing a Stronger Sense of Self

"Owning our story and, loving ourselves through that process, is the bravest thing that we'll ever do" – Brené Brown

Having a positive self-identity means having a strong and confident sense of self-worth and self-respect, a deep understanding and acceptance of our values, beliefs, strengths, and weaknesses.

It's about having an approach to life with a

sense of purpose, confidence, and optimism.

It means pursuing our goals and dreams with resilience and determination, and knowing that we are valuable and deserving of good things like love, respect, and success.

It's about recognizing our own worth and believing in ourselves, and seeing ourselves as capable, worthy, and deserving, and embracing our unique qualities with confidence.

Developing a positive self-identity involves a journey of self-discovery and self-acceptance. It requires us to challenge negative self-talk and limiting beliefs that may be holding us back, and replacing them with positive affirmations and beliefs that empower us. We may also need to surround ourselves with positive and supportive people who encourage us to be our best selves.

When we have a positive self-identity, we are more likely to pursue our goals and dreams with enthusiasm and to handle life's challenges with resilience and grace. We are also more likely to attract positive relationships and experiences into our lives and to live a life that is true to our authentic selves.

Ways for you cultivate a positive self-identity are:

- *Have confidence in your abilities and worth.*
- *Accept your flaws and imperfections.*
- *Have a clear sense of your personal values.*
- *Have resilience in the face of challenges.*
- *Embrace your unique qualities.*

- **Have confidence in your abilities and worth**: Believe in yourself and your abilities, and recognize your strengths and accomplishments. It's easy to get caught up in self-doubt and negative self-talk, but it's important to remember that you are capable and worthy.

  By having confidence in yourself and recognizing your worth, you can cultivate a positive self-image and boost your self-esteem. This can lead to greater success in all areas of your life, including your career, relationships, and personal growth. So take the time to appreciate your strengths and accomplishments, and believe in yourself and your abilities!

Practice positive-self talk: Instead of saying 'I can't do this', try saying 'I am capable' and 'I can do this'.

Celebrate your achievements: Recognize your successes and accomplishments, no matter how big or small they may be. Celebrate them and take pride in what you have achieved.

Set realistic goals: Setting achievable goals can help build confidence and a sense of accomplishment. When you meet your goals, you'll feel a sense of pride and satisfaction.

Learn new skills: Learning new skills and taking on new challenges can help you build confidence in your abilities. You may discover hidden talents or strengths that you didn't know you had.

Don't compare yourself to others: Remember that everyone has their own unique journey and accomplishments. Comparing yourself to others can be harmful and can undermine your confidence.

Let go of the need for approval: Seeking praise or validation from others can, unfortunately, come at the expense of your own needs. Everyone has different perspectives, biases, and expectations, which means that seeking validation from others is an endless and ultimately unsatisfying pursuit. Remember, it's important to prioritize your own well-being and values.

Stop worrying what others think of you: When you worry too much about what others think of you, you are essentially giving them power over your life and emotions. You're trying to control something that's ultimately out of your control. No matter how hard you try to please others or mold yourself to fit their expectations, there will always be someone who thinks you're great, or someone who disapproves or has a negative opinion of you. You cannot please everyone so, instead of focusing on others opinions, shift your focus back to yourself and know that you are perfect just as you are.

- **Accept your flaws and imperfections:** It's important to remember that nobody is perfect. We all have flaws and imperfections that make us unique. However, it can be easy to feel ashamed or insecure about these aspects of ourselves. Instead of allowing these negative emotions to consume us, it's important to learn to accept our flaws and imperfections.

Accepting our imperfections involves treating ourselves with kindness and empathy when striving for self-improvement, instead of harsh self-judgment and criticism. When we acknowledge and accept our flaws, we can release the negative emotions that hinder our progress and channel our energy towards creating constructive changes in our lives.

Remember, we are all works in progress. We will make mistakes, have weaknesses, and face challenges throughout our lives. But by accepting our flaws and imperfections, we can learn to love ourselves for who we are and work towards becoming the best version of ourselves. *(See Chapter 11)*

- **Have a clear sense of your personal values:** It's important to have a clear understanding of your personal values. These values are unique to each person and can include things like honesty, integrity, kindness, respect, and perseverance. When you have a strong sense of your personal values, you can use them as a compass to navigate through life's challenges and make choices that align with your beliefs.

When your values are in line with your actions, you will feel a greater sense of purpose and meaning in your life. For example, if you value honesty, you'll feel good about being truthful with others, even if it's difficult. Similarly, if you value kindness, you'll feel fulfilled by doing things that help others. This sense of purpose and meaning can give you a sense of direction in life and help you feel more fulfilled.

Living in alignment with your values can also help you develop a stronger sense of self. When you know what's important to you and act accordingly, you'll have a clearer understanding of who you are and what you stand for. This can boost your confidence and help you feel more grounded in your identity.

Here are some ways to help you gain a clear sense of your personal values:

- *Self-reflection:* Take some time to reflect on your life experiences and the decisions you have made. Ask yourself what matters to you the most and what motivates you. Think about the moments when you felt happiest or most fulfilled and try to identify the values that were present in those moments.

- *Write it down:* Make a list of the values that are most important to you. It can be helpful to use a values list as a starting point and then narrow down the list to the values that truly resonate with you. Once you have your list, prioritize them in order of importance.

- *Seek feedback:* Talk to people who know you well, such as friends or family members, and ask them what values they see in you. This can provide valuable insight into your own values and help you to see yourself from a different perspective.

- *Take a values assessment:* There are many online assessments that can help you identify your personal values. These assessments typically ask you a series of questions and then provide you with a list of values that match your responses. You can use this list as a starting point for further exploration.

- *Identify your non-negotiables:* Think about the values that you are not willing to compromise on. These are the values that are so important to you that you would be willing to make sacrifices in order to uphold them. Identifying your non-negotiables can help you to gain a clear sense of your personal values and priorities.

  - **Have resilience in the face of challenges:** When facing challenges or setbacks in life, it's important to have resilience. Resilience means being able to bounce back and keep going even when things get tough. Instead of letting challenges define your self-worth, it's important to view them as opportunities for growth. By doing this, you can learn from your experiences and become stronger as a result. It's easy to feel defeated when things don't go according to plan, but having resilience can help you stay focused and motivated despite any setbacks that come your way.

Here are ways to help you learn to have resilience in the face of challenges:

- *Focus on the solution, not the problem*: Instead of dwelling on what went wrong, focus on what you can do to fix the situation. This can help you feel more in control and less overwhelmed by the challenge.

- *Seek support*: Don't be afraid to ask for help when you need it. Reach out to friends, family, or a therapist for support and guidance. Having a support system can help you feel less alone and more empowered to overcome challenges.

- *Stay positive*: Try to maintain a positive outlook, even when things get tough. Focus on the good things in your life and look for the silver lining in difficult situations. This can help you stay motivated and hopeful, even when facing challenges.

- *Learn from your experiences*: Every challenge is an opportunity to learn and grow. Take time to reflect on what you've learned from the experience and how you can use that knowledge to improve in the future. This can help you build resilience and feel more confident in your ability to handle challenges.

Remember, challenges are a natural part of life, and it's how you respond to them that ultimately determines your success. So stay positive, keep moving forward, and have faith in your ability to overcome any obstacle that comes your way.

- **Embrace your unique qualities**: Embracing your unique qualities is essential to building a positive self-identity. It's easy to get caught up in societal norms and expectations, but when you learn to embrace what makes you unique, you unlock a whole new level of self-confidence and self-love. Your quirks, passions, flaws, and individual perspectives all contribute to your sense of self, and it's important to celebrate these aspects of yourself rather than suppress them. By embracing your uniqueness, you can live authentically and connect more deeply with yourself and others.

- *Embrace your quirks*: Don't try to hide or suppress the things that make you unique, even if they may seem unusual or quirky. Instead, celebrate these qualities and let them shine.

- *Explore your passions*: Pursue the things that make you happy and passionate, whether it's a hobby, a creative pursuit, or a cause that you care about. Embracing your passions can help you feel more connected to yourself and your sense of purpose.

- *Accept your flaws*: No one is perfect, and accepting your flaws and imperfections can actually help you build a stronger sense of self-acceptance and self-worth. Instead of trying to hide or deny your flaws, work on accepting them as a natural part of who you are.

- *Practice self-expression*: Find ways to express yourself authentically, whether it's through art, writing, music, or any other medium that speaks to you. Expressing yourself creatively can help you feel more confident and empowered in your sense of self.

- *Surround yourself with diversity*: Seek out people who come from different backgrounds, cultures, and perspectives. This can help you broaden your own understanding of the world and embrace the diversity that makes us all unique.

"You Are a Badass" by Jen Sincero, is a great book that helps you embrace your unique qualities and build confidence. It's written in a fun style, with relatable stories and practical advice to help you step out of your comfort zone and pursue your dreams. The author wants you to embrace your badass qualities - that's the unique things that make you awesome - and stop doubting your greatness. She covers all sorts of topics, like getting rid of limiting beliefs, practicing gratitude, and taking risks. The book is written in a way that makes you feel like you're hanging out with a wise and funny friend.........

When you work on building a stronger sense of who you are, it's not just good for you - it also helps you build better relationships with others. By treating yourself with kindness and respect, and knowing what you need and want, you'll develop a better relationship with yourself. And when you feel good about yourself, you're less likely to feel lonely, and more likely to attract positive people into your life. So, don't forget to invest in yourself - it'll pay off in all sorts of ways!

For me it involves consistently working on accepting myself just the way I am, flaws and all, while still striving for self-improvement without dwelling on my mistakes. It also means having a clear understanding of my personal values and using them as a guide when making decisions. Whenever I encounter setbacks, I always view them as opportunities for growth.

It's important to recognize that building a stronger self-identity is a process. The journey may be challenging at times, but the rewards will be well worth the effort.

16. FINDING YOUR PASSION AND PURPOSE
How to Live a Meaningful Life

"The two most important days in your life are the day you are born and the day you find out why." - Mark Twain

I think that discovering your passion and purpose is like finding a magic key that unlocks the door to overcoming loneliness.

You might feel like you've already tackled a lot of the issues discussed in this book, but there may still be something missing. That's where discovering your passion and purpose comes in. When you're doing something that you truly love and feel passionate about, it can bring so much joy into your life.

When we talk about finding our passion and purpose in life, we are referring to the process of discovering the things that truly inspire and motivate us, and aligning our lives with those things. This involves identifying our core values, interests, strengths, and desires, and exploring how we can use those qualities to make a positive impact in the world.

For me, writing is that thing. It keeps me busy and engaged in something that brings me genuine happiness and, because I'm so busy pursuing my passion, I don't have as much time to feel lonely or isolated. It has been a significant factor in helping me overcome my own feelings of loneliness.

Take some time to explore what you're truly passionate about. It's not always an easy task. It can take a lot of self-reflection, exploration, and experimentation to find out what truly drives and motivates you.

You may need to face your fears and challenge your beliefs, but the process can be incredibly rewarding and empowering. It can help you discover new opportunities and possibilities, and connect with a sense of purpose and meaning that can guide you through life's ups and downs.

It's important to note that it is an ongoing process that may require experimentation, reflection, and adjustment over time.

Please know that it is okay if your first attempt doesn't work out because it's all part of the journey. Every experience is a stepping stone that will lead you closer to your ultimate destination. Don't be afraid to try new things, and don't be afraid to let go of something that doesn't work out. It's all part of the process of finding what truly resonates with you and what you are meant to do. Remember that each step, even if it seems like a misstep, is still leading you towards your purpose. So keep trying, keep exploring, and trust that you'll eventually find your way.

When we stay open to new experiences and opportunities, and when we make a commitment to aligning our lives with our purpose and values, we can build a more fulfilling and purpose-driven life, and overcome feelings of loneliness and isolation.

Finding your passion and purpose in life is a deeply personal and individual process, there is no one-size-fits-all approach. However, here are some general strategies that can help you identify your passions and align them with your purpose:

Explore your interests: Begin by exploring your interests and hobbies, and pay attention to the activities that bring you joy. Ask yourself what you are naturally drawn to, and try new things to see what resonates with you. This can help you uncover new passions or rediscover old ones.

Consider your values: Reflect on your values and what is important to you in life. This can help you identify activities and causes that align with your values and give your life greater meaning and purpose.

Identify your strengths: Take some time to reflect on your skills and strengths, and think about how you can use them to make a positive impact in the world. Consider how you can use your unique talents to help others or contribute to a cause you care about.

Pay attention to your intuition: Listen to your inner voice and pay attention to your intuition. This can help you connect with your true desires and passions, and give you a sense of direction in your life.

Try new things: Sometimes we don't know what we're passionate about until we try something new. Take a class, join a club, or sign up for a workshop in a topic you're curious about. You might discover a new passion or interest that you never knew you had.

Seek inspiration: Look for inspiration from others who are following their passions and living a purposeful life. Read books, watch documentaries, and seek out mentors or role models who can provide guidance and support.

Talk to others: Ask friends and family members what they think your strengths and passions are. Sometimes others may see things in us that we don't see in ourselves.

Volunteer: Volunteering can be a great way to discover your passion and purpose. By helping others, you may discover a cause that you're passionate about and want to dedicate your time and energy to.

Below are three books you might be interested in when looking to find your passion and purpose:

1. _"How to Build a Well-Lived, Joyful Life" by Bill Burnett and Dave Evans._

This is an amazing book that can help anyone who is looking to find their passion and purpose in life. It's written by two Stanford University professors, Bill Burnett and Dave Evans, and they share practical strategies to design and build a fulfilling life.

The book is divided into three parts, which are easy to follow and understand. In the first part, readers learn how to clarify their values and goals, and identify their strengths and weaknesses. In the second part, they'll discover how to use design thinking to prototype and test different life paths. And in the third part, they'll get guidance on how to implement and iterate their chosen life design.

What I love about this book is that it's not just theoretical. Burnett and Evans provide real-life examples and stories from people who have successfully used design thinking to build a joyful life. The book also includes practical exercises, worksheets, and checklists to help readers apply the concepts discussed in each chapter.

Overall it's is a great read for anyone who wants to take control of their life and create a future that aligns with their values and aspirations.

2. *"Big Magic" by Elizabeth Gilbert*

   In her book, Elizabeth Gilbert encourages people to tap into their creativity and unleash their inner artist. She believes that, by focusing on creativity, people can discover new passions and purposes that they may not have even known existed. Gilbert suggests that the act of creating can be a form of self-discovery, as it allows people to explore their thoughts, feelings, and ideas in a meaningful way.

   Overall, Big Magic is a book that celebrates the power of creativity and encourages readers to embrace their inner artist. While it may not provide a step-by-step guide to finding your passion and purpose, it can help you to tap into your creativity and discover new possibilities for your life.

3. <u>"The Alchemist" by Paulo Coelho.</u>

    This is one of my favourite books. It's about a boy named Santiago who wants to find a treasure in Egypt. He meets different people along the way, and learns important lessons about life.

    The book teaches us to follow our dreams and listen to our heart. Santiago learns that he should pursue his life's purpose even if it's hard. The book also says that everything in the universe is connected, and we can use a spiritual force to achieve our goals. The message of the book is to follow your dreams and live a life that has meaning and purpose.

Remember, finding your passion and purpose in life is an ongoing process that may require patience and perseverance. It's important to approach this journey with an open mind and heart and, as always, be kind and compassionate to yourself along the way.

17. PRACTICING GRATITUDE
The Transformative Power of Appreciation

"If you only say one prayer a day, make it Thank You" - Rumi

Gratitude is when we take a moment to appreciate the good things in our lives. It's about feeling thankful and appreciative for the people, experiences, and things that make our lives better. Practicing gratitude can be seriously powerful, especially when we're feeling alone.

When we're going through a tough time and feeling isolated, it can be easy to focus on the negative and forget about all the good things in our lives. But, by intentionally practicing gratitude, we can shift our focus and start to see all the amazing people and experiences around us that we might have been overlooking before.

By taking the time to recognize the people who have touched our lives in small ways, like a kind word from a stranger or a smile from someone passing by, it can help us feel more connected and grateful.

And, the best thing about practicing gratitude is it can act as a magnet, attracting more positive experiences, people and opportunities into our lives!

According to the law of attraction, the reason for this is because the energy and thoughts we put out into the universe, through gratitude, create a positive vibration that attracts similar energy back to us.

By focusing on the things we are thankful for, we create a sense of abundance and joy within ourselves, which can then attract more abundance and joy into our lives. It's like a positive feedback loop - the more we practice gratitude, the more positive experiences and opportunities we attract, which then give us even more to be grateful for.

So, if you're looking to improve your life and attract more positivity and abundance, practicing gratitude is a great place to start. By simply taking a few minutes each day to reflect on the things you are thankful for, you will begin to see a positive shift taking place.

A top choice for me on the power of practicing gratitude is *"The Gratitude Diaries" by Janice Kaplan*. In this book, the author shares her personal experiences, and research, on the benefits of gratitude, including how it can improve our relationships, health, and overall happiness.

Janice Kaplan writes: *"Gratitude is a powerful force. It can transform our lives by helping us focus on what we have, rather than what we lack. It can improve our relationships by making us more appreciative of the people in our lives. It can even improve our health by reducing stress and promoting a more positive outlook.*

But practicing gratitude isn't always easy. We live in a culture that often emphasizes material success and achievement over simple pleasures and everyday joys. We're bombarded with messages that tell us we need more in order to be happy.

That's why cultivating gratitude requires intention and effort. It's not enough to simply say we're grateful for something – we need to actively seek out and appreciate the good things in our lives. We need to make gratitude a habit, something we do regularly and intentionally.

One way to do this is by keeping a gratitude journal. Each day, write down three things you're grateful for. They can be big or small, significant or mundane – what matters is that you take the time to appreciate them. This simple practice can help shift your focus from what's lacking to what's present, and over time, can transform your outlook on life."

Below are some examples of how we can practice gratitude:

- *Keep a Gratitude Journal*: Every day, take a moment to jot down three, or more, things that you're grateful for. It can be anything, big or small, from the gorgeous cup of coffee you had that morning to the support of a loved one. The key is to really take the time to appreciate these things and reflect on how they make you feel.

- *Express gratitude to others*: Remember to show your appreciation to those who have made a positive impact on your life. It could be a friend who's always there for you, a family member who's given you valuable advice, a co-worker who's helped you out on a project, or even a stranger who's done something kind for you. Take a moment to thank them and let them know how much they mean to you. It doesn't have to be anything fancy - a simple message or a heartfelt conversation can go a long way in making someone's day and strengthening your relationships.

- *Practice mindfulness*: Take a step back and appreciate the present moment. Take a moment to slow down and really notice the world around you - the colour of the sky, the sounds of nature, the feeling of the sun on your skin. Taking just a few moments to appreciate the present can bring a sense of calm and contentment. So, breathe in the fresh air, listen to the birds chirping, and savour the little moments that make life so special.

- *Count your blessings*: Take a moment to count your blessings and make a list of all the things in your life that you're grateful for. It could be the people who love and support you, the experiences that have shaped you, the possessions that bring you comfort, or anything else that fills you with joy. There's no right or wrong answer - just focus on the things that make your heart full and your life richer. And don't worry if your list starts out short - you might be surprised at how much there is to be grateful for once you start paying attention!

- *Focus on what you have, not what you lack*: It's easy to get caught up in what we don't have, but it's important to shift our focus to what we do have. Take a moment to appreciate the abundance in your life, no matter how small it may seem. Maybe it's the roof over your head, the food in your fridge, or even the simple pleasures like a good book or a warm bath. Instead of dwelling on what you lack, focus on what you have and how it enriches your life.

Writing down these moments of gratitude can be a fantastic reminder that we have so much abundance, that we're not alone, and that there are people all around us who actually *are* making a positive impact on our lives, even if it's in small ways.

That feeling of truly appreciating everything that's around us can be incredibly uplifting and inspiring. And, as a result, help us to feel less alone and more connected to the world around us.

So, if you're feeling alone, I would definitely recommend taking some time to focus on gratitude. You might be surprised at how much better it can make you feel.

18. SEEKING PROFESSIONAL HELP
How Therapy can Help you Overcome Loneliness

"Sometimes the bravest and most important thing you can do is just show up and let someone else help you". – Michelle Obama

I sincerely hope that this book has been helpful in easing any feelings of loneliness you may be experiencing. However, because loneliness can be a challenging and painful experience, and if you find that you are still struggling and unable to overcome it, I recommend seeking professional help.

One way to get help for loneliness is to talk to your doctor who may be able to refer you to a professional who specializes in loneliness or related issues.

If you have health insurance, you can check with your provider to see if they cover mental health services. Many plans now offer coverage for therapy and counselling sessions. You can also request a list of in-network mental health providers in your area. This can help you find a professional who accepts your insurance and is conveniently located.

You can also try finding therapy services online. There are lots of websites and apps that provide virtual counselling sessions with licensed therapists. This can be a really handy and budget-friendly option, especially if you can't access in-person services or would rather have therapy sessions online. Plus, you can stay anonymous if that's what you prefer.

When you talk to a therapist, they create a safe and welcoming space for you to talk about your feelings. They can help you understand why you feel lonely and teach you ways to cope with those feelings.

There are several options available to you, depending on your preferences and needs.

Below are some of the most commonly used therapies:

- ***Cognitive-Behavioural Therapy (CBT):*** CBT is a type of talk therapy that can help individuals identify and challenge negative thought patterns and behaviours that may contribute to their feelings of loneliness. The therapist will work with the person to develop coping strategies and more positive ways of thinking about themselves and their relationships with others.

- ***Interpersonal Therapy (IPT)***: IPT is a type of therapy that focuses on improving social skills and interpersonal relationships. The therapist helps the person identify and address any issues that may be affecting their ability to connect with others, such as difficulty making or maintaining friendships.

- ***Group Therapy:*** Group therapy involves meeting with a therapist and other individuals who are also struggling with loneliness. The group provides a safe and supportive environment where individuals can share their experiences and feelings with others who understand what they're going through. The group can also provide feedback, support, and encouragement to one another.

- **_Mindfulness-Based Therapies:_** Mindfulness-based therapies, such as mindfulness-based stress reduction (MBSR), can help individuals learn to be more present and aware of their thoughts and emotions. This can be particularly helpful for individuals struggling with loneliness, as it can help them better understand and cope with their feelings.

- **_Art Therapy:_** Art therapy can be a helpful way for individuals to express their emotions and explore their feelings of loneliness through creative expression. A trained art therapist can guide the person through the process and provide support and feedback.

It's important to keep in mind that there is no single therapy approach that works for everyone, and what may work for one person may not work for another. Therefore, it's important to consult a mental health professional to figure out which type of therapy may be best suited for your individual needs and preferences.

If you are feeling hesitant about seeking professional help for loneliness, this is completely normal. You might worry that people will judge you, or think that you should be able to cope with your feelings on your own. You might also be worried about the cost of therapy or feel unsure about how to find a therapist who can help you.

It's important to remember that seeking professional help for loneliness is a brave and important step towards feeling better. Loneliness is a common feeling, and there is no shame in seeking help to manage it. A therapist can provide a safe and supportive space for you to explore your feelings and develop coping strategies to manage them. Take your time and find the right therapist who you feel comfortable talking to.

19. MAINTAINING LONG-TERM WELLBEING
How to Build a Supportive Lifestyle

"Surround yourself with only people who are going to lift you higher" – Oprah

As we come to the end of our journey together, I want to express my heartfelt appreciation to you for joining me in exploring the many facets of loneliness and how we can overcome it.

I hope that this book has been a source of comfort and inspiration for you, and that you have found practical guidance and tools to help you navigate the challenges of loneliness.

In this book, we have delved into the causes and effects of loneliness, and discovered tools and techniques to help us build self-love and acceptance, silence our inner critic, cultivate mindfulness and self-compassion, and connect with others.

Through cognitive restructuring, nurturing our inner child, and managing social anxiety, we have learned how to break the cycle of isolation and fear, and embrace forgiveness and vulnerability as powerful tools for healing and growth.

We have also explored the dangers of perfectionism and the importance of developing a positive self-identity, finding our passion and purpose, and practicing gratitude as a way to transform our lives.

Throughout this journey, I have emphasized the importance of seeking professional help when needed. Therapy can provide invaluable support in overcoming loneliness, and can help you to develop the tools and skills needed to live a happier, more fulfilling life.

But, how do you ensure that these positive changes are sustainable in the long term? How do you make sure that you don't fall back into old patterns of thought and behaviour?

The answer lies in developing habits and routines that support your overall wellbeing. Here are some tips to help you stay on track:

Prioritize self-care: Remember to take care of yourself both physically and mentally. This means getting enough sleep, eating well, exercising regularly, and practicing self-compassion.

Stay connected: Don't let your newfound social connections fall by the wayside. Make an effort to stay in touch with the people who matter to you, whether that's through phone calls, text messages, or in-person meetups.

Set boundaries: It's important to know your limits and to respect them. Don't be afraid to say no to activities or people that drain your energy or compromise your values.

Practice mindfulness: Keep up with your mindfulness practice, whether that's through meditation, yoga, or simply taking moments throughout the day to pause and breathe.

Keep learning and growing: Continue to seek out new experiences, learn new skills, and challenge yourself in healthy ways. This can help prevent boredom and stagnation, and keep you engaged and fulfilled.

Seek support when needed: Don't be afraid to reach out for help when you need it. Whether that's through therapy, support groups, or simply talking to a trusted friend or family member, it's important to have a support system in place.

Sustaining your wellbeing is a lifelong journey, and it's okay to stumble along the way. The key is to stay committed to your goals, stay open to new experiences and perspectives and, more importantly, be kind and compassionate towards yourself every step of the way.

Remember, you are not alone in your journey, and with patience, connection, and self-love, you can overcome loneliness and create a life filled with meaning, purpose, and joy. Practice self-love every day, and watch as it transforms your life from the inside out.

And, hopefully one day, you too will find yourself giving a thanks to loneliness.

ABOUT THE AUTHOR

Mary Bridget O'Brien is a writer based in Spain, originally from Ireland. She has always had a passion for helping others, and has spent many years studying and practicing self-reflection and personal growth techniques.

A Thanks to Loneliness is Mary Bridget's debut book, born from her personal journey of self-discovery. As someone who never thought she would feel gratitude for having experienced loneliness, Mary Bridget is thrilled to share the tools and insights that helped her come through the other side. In A Thanks to Loneliness, she explores the power of vulnerability, self-reflection, and gratitude, offering readers practical strategies for finding purpose and meaning in their own struggles.

When Mary Bridget isn't writing, she enjoys swimming, practicing yoga, and experimenting in the kitchen. She is also an avid reader and loves exploring new cultures and cuisines.

Printed in Dunstable, United Kingdom